QUIT WHILE YOU'RE A-HEAD

(Terrifying Tales of a Teesside Teacher)

PUBLISHING

First Edition published 2018 by
2QT Limited (Publishing)
Settle, North Yorkshire BD24 9RH United Kingdom

Printed in Great Britain by Lightning Source UK Ltd
A CIP catalogue record for this book is available
from the British Library

ISBN 978-1-912014-11-8

QUIT WHILE YOU'RE A-HEAD

(Terrifying Tales of a Teesside Teacher)

Bryan Cross

Dedication

My thanks to staff and pupils, too numerous to mention, from so many schools for so many years, especially those from the following:

Thornaby Village Infant (now Primary)

Queen Street Junior, Thornaby (now demolished!)

Billingham North Junior (now Pentland Primary)

The Firs Preparatory School, Nunthorpe (now closed!)

Brambles Farm Junior (now Primary), Middlesbrough

Frederick Nattrass Junior (now Primary), Norton-on-Tees

Fens Junior and Primary, Hartlepool

Grange Junior and Primary, Hartlepool

Oxbridge Primary, Stockton-on-Tees

Tilery Primary, Stockton-on-Tees

But especially thanks to my wife Linda Elizabeth, sons Matty and Mark, and daughters-in-law Danika and Sarah. Thanks, guys, for your love, care, support and sacrifice.

Plus my late brother and wife Arthur and Alice, brother Don and wife Sheila, sister Doreen and her late husband Dick, together with all their families for an ever-open door to share my 'troubles'.

Also great friends Steve Brannigan and Carole Prichard – caring and loving people – along with so many others from Stockton-on-Tees and Hartlepool, and recently from Castleton, North Yorkshire and adjoining villages.

Oh, and Beth Thirlwall, who will disown me if I don't give her a mention!

Thank you.

Foreword

It was such a long time ago when I attended FNJ&I mixed school. That's Frederick Nattrass Junior and Infants mixed school, now a fully amalgamated primary school, known locally then as now as 'Freddy Natt'!

After being a pupil there, I had the good fortune to move to Blakeston Comprehensive School then on to play professional football with Billingham Town, Middlesbrough (The Boro), Manchester United and the England senior team. But it all started way back at Freddy Natt.

Football coaching at the school was given by a young teacher, Mr Bryan Cross ('Crossy'), who as I recall had boundless energy and enthusiasm, giving us his time not only in games and PE lessons but after school, Saturday mornings and even at lunchtimes. So my football education, so to speak, began in that school in Norton-on Tees.

Having played alongside so many famous players such as Eric Cantona, Ryan Giggs, Bryan Robson, Paul Scholes, etc. from Man Utd, and local 'Boro' stars such as Tony Mowbray and Bernie Slaven, throughout the years in many parts of the world we have all shared one thing in common: someone started us off on our career and gave us a platform and opportunity.

So, with that in mind, I'm grateful to Bryan (Crossy) for his time and the opportunity to play football. He wasn't the only one, of course, but until I was about ten years of age he was my first football 'boss'.

To hundreds of pupils he provided happy, fun and enjoyable football coaching sessions, including practice and school matches, so it is with great affection and thanks I write a short introduction to his book. In one sense it is a recognition of so many sports teachers, past and present who gave – and give – of their time, expertise and enthusiasm to develop sport within youngsters, boys and girls alike.

I trust this book will awaken memories for many ex-pupils in all schools – but especially those who played on Bluehall Rec and the Freddy Natt school football pitch.

Thanks.
Gary Pallister

Contents

INTRODUCTION

So where to begin chronicling my adventures through a lifetime, so it seems, in school? *Why* have I chosen to chronicle them? Well, as someone once remarked, 'never work with animals or children'.

James Herriot (veterinary surgeon and author) told his tales of life in North Yorkshire and, if I recall correctly, seemed to enjoy and survive his experiences with animals, so I'll have a go at the 'two-legged beasties'! To be honest, I don't aspire to a readership of James Herriot's proportions.

If you are reading this, in all probability you have been taught somewhere by someone who was a teacher. Those who have been 'schooled' in any sense of the word may find my simple words amusing. This book will also try to explain to my own children why Dad displayed such odd behaviour on far too many occasions!

Interestingly enough, my school memoirs may well be the only proof that the schools I attended existed. The infant school I went to changed its name and was completely modernised; school number two was demolished; school three changed its name, and number four (my 'prep' school) just disappeared. The college where I studied for my Higher National Diploma has recently been flattened for housing development.

But there's more... My teacher-training college has also been knocked down; both the junior schools where I taught for almost twenty years have changed status to become primary schools. Finally, to cap it all, the primary school from which I retired as head teacher was burnt to the ground a few short months after I left (missed me, ha-ha!!). As I finish writing this introduction, Brambles School in Middlesbrough in which I had my first experience of teaching practice has just had an arson attack and two classrooms have been gutted. How's that for covering one's tracks?

Although few educational establishments have remained the same following my departure (did I hear someone mention 'the kiss of death'), I have at least acquired a fund of memories that will stay with me forever, in spite of me trying my very best to erase some of the best-forgotten ones from my mind.

To quote the Scottish bard Robbie Burns: ' *Oh the gift that God would give us to see ourselves as others see us*'. Close behind would be the gift of seeing things through a child's eyes. Second-guessing the way children view things in and out of school is a skill that very few teachers possess. Sadly, if they're not careful, even the most experienced members of staff can too readily assume they know how children tick. Hardened by hundreds of ex-pupils, they lose sight of the wonderment and joy of some youngsters who cross our thresholds for the first time, or even after a break away from school.

This was brought home to me quite sharply on one occasion when, on a bright September morning with a heavy heart (I was returning after the long summer holiday), I chastised a boy for leaping about in his class line.

'Stop being silly, young man,' I barked. 'What is wrong with you?'

'It's just great to be back in school, sir!' he replied.

Happily the boy in question really meant it and his reply was in sharp contrast to the sarcastic comments the teaching staff had been muttering earlier in the morning: 'Isn't it great to be back?'… 'Oh, happy day!'

So, I hope you enjoy reading my book. If it makes you smile, recall a memory of your own schooldays or consider for a moment the world that exists behind the school wall, it wouldn't surprise me one little bit!

1
Bottoms Up

'I LIKE CHILDREN –
I USED TO GO TO SCHOOL WITH THEM.'

Tommy Cooper

Those who can, do; those who can't, teach! Possibly, very possibly indeed; after all, most of us have been through the school system and we've all experienced being taught in all its varied, painful or pleasurable permutations.

Thankfully the break from school comes to all of us, although some of us return when our children start attending school, when we become adult learners or, as I did, to teach. Of course, there are those who are encapsulated in the system from an early age and never return to the 'normal' world. School–college–school; there are legions of teachers hooked on the heady stuff of chalk (now board markers), fresh sawdust for the 'sickie' children, polished hall floors, etc. These are what I call the 'schoolies': poor unfortunates who have never known life other than in school, save for the occasional holiday work as Christmas 'posties', holiday-camp waiting staff, casual labourers or workers on supermarket check-outs.

For almost ten years I was absent from this mysterious world of school only to be enticed back – I was never going to be a captain of industry at ICI – via that enchanting institution, the teacher-training college. So, I entered that child-centred, childlike and often childish (but the secret will remain with me, guys!) establishment, never to emerge with the same perspectives as before.

*

Perhaps those of you familiar with jostling with plastic carrier bags from the shops (I do hope you are a 'bag for life, save the planet' type of person – see, it's the 'teacher telling you', coming out in me!) will understand what happens on the student teachers' bus. Instead of tins of beans, packs of cereals and 10p off super-savers, there are rolled-up maps, bags of toilet roll insides, scores of empty margarine tubs or egg boxes and perhaps, for good measure a stuffed armadillo! Yes, it's the student teachers' bus disgorging an army of 'academic ants' to busy themselves on their teaching practice.

After three weeks, four weeks or even six weeks (if the school is unlucky!), the teacher-training students are released on the unsuspecting pupils – or perhaps the reverse. The pupils are ready and waiting to feast on the students. It's a surprising fact of life but the disruptive, unruly children and the 'Please, sir/miss, what do we do now?' brigade can spot a student teacher from a whole playground's distance, even on the foggiest, coldest winter morning. In truth, students are as discernable as a pork pie and a jar of pickled onions on a table at a badminton-club buffet. With their bright college scarves and nervous twitch, armed to the teeth with teaching aids, the poor students are off like proverbial lambs to the slaughter.

No matter how experienced or raw the recruit, all those in the teaching profession have had their moments in the deep end; in spite of how gentle and gradual the phasing in, there comes that spine-chilling moment when you're in front of a class for the first time. Pupils' pupils gaze at you, watching every move, observing the slightest flaw – button undone, make-up smudged, ladder in tights or collar uneven. I have known students be physically sick, dry up – and I know of one young lady who fainted in front of her class within minutes! Don't mock the students; when I was a head, a smart-suited bank manager from a high-street bank turned round to me whilst addressing the whole school and, sweating profusely (is there any other way to sweat?), said, 'I don't think I can do this!'

Indeed, I was similarly placed when, one fine autumn morning, I was despatched to my first practice school, a junior school in deepest, downtown Middlesbrough. I was accompanied by another guinea pig, who was dropped off not by the students' bus but from another student's car. It's surprising how much you can cram into the back of an Austin A40!

In a mood not far removed from those who went out from the trenches, I braced myself and entered through the doors. There followed the introduction to the venerable body of teachers in the small, cramped staffroom and, in the blur of faces, timetables on the wall, union posters hanging by a solitary drawing pin and a tray of assorted mugs, I met Mr P.

A teacher of many years experience, Mr P. was also a veteran biker, possessing leather helmet, World War I goggles and gauntlets more suited to a giant's hands. In Mr P.'s wake, I moved to the classroom. Let me say that he was an excellent teacher and his control and discipline with a class of forty-plus (yes that's four-zero – classes were huge in those days) eight to nine year olds was quite superb. In fact, he was so good that I was fooled into thinking it was easy.

Two days of observation and it was my turn to go solo.

I had discovered a marvellous poem about autumn, beautifully illustrated, and so I began. Mr P., my mentor, had made some excuse to collect some paper from the stock cupboard. Perhaps the anticipated merriment of the floorshow that was about to begin was just too much for him.

Perched nonchalantly against his desk, I delivered the poem in a smooth and polished fashion – well, I had been rehearsing for at least a month! You could have heard a pin drop. What a performance!

'Now, class, did you enjoy that poem?'

Silence

'Come on, don't be shy. What words tell you about the autumn season? Shall we write some autumn words on the board?'

A hand went up. An answer, a question – whatever, it was a response!

'Yes, young lady.'

And Barbara – I can picture her now, a very thin girl wearing red woolly tights, a grey skirt and a navy jumper – replied… 'Please, sir, I like your trousers!'

Things went steadily downhill that morning and a very fit, young teacher-training student left the school at 4.15pm absolutely shredded, worked over and soundly pummelled by a group of eight to nine year olds. Head pounding, with thoughts of 'How am I possibly going to manage tomorrow?', I bundled my way into the car that was giving me a lift and headed for the nearest bottle of aspirin. But, maybe to the regret of hundreds of future pupils, I did manage to return the following day and in spite of numerous difficulties did, to quote Tina Turner, survive!

*

My next practice, and believe me I was practising, was in a secondary school and here too I made a memorable first impression. It was a typical Monday morning, second session with a class of Year 7 twelve year olds. A swimming lesson at the baths, how lovely! How I adore swimming – well, not really; I am to swimming what Prince Charles is to sumo wrestling!

However, I was keen to impress, so suitably clad in a borrowed costume (this was a great mistake) I entered the poolside – slim, athletic and freezing cold. While the instructor and PE teacher were discussing the forthcoming activities and registering the class, I thought I'd swim a width across the baths to observe the pupils' warm-up session. In actual fact, I wanted them to see that I had gained my ten-metres swimming certificate.

Halfway across the pool I came to grief; it is difficult to swim with trunks around your ankles! Borrowing my dad's all-woollen trunks, as I mentioned earlier, was indeed a great mistake. Oh, help! In the thrashing of water that followed, I regained my sad costume and a certain amount of composure and splashed my way across to the side. Strangely, there was no laughter and no comments; I'm sure the class were already busy planning devious deeds to inflict upon this daring young student who showed such barefaced cheek!

At the end of the first week things were going quite well, so I thought. Incidents arose but somehow I managed to cope. One such incident occurred when I had to question a boy called Michael, just a very simple routine maths question. Thinking he hadn't heard me, I repeated the question; again he did not reply so I walked over to his desk in the front row. 'Do you understand, Michael?' I asked.

Slowly he uncoiled and stood. I swear his legs must have been concertinaed underneath his chair, as he rose and rose towards the ceiling. At least six feet plus, he looked down at all five feet eight inches of me and said, 'You don't frighten me.'

In reply I said, 'Good, Michael, I'm pleased because that's the last thing I want to do…' muttering under my breath '…if I'm to live.' Then I rapidly retreated and, with a quickening pulse, continued my lesson.

*

Fellow students had many tales to exchange during these hectic periods of teaching practice. I was in awe of one of my peer group, John, when I heard of his whole-school involvement. He had set up an animal day, with his class bringing in their pets – rabbits, dogs, cats, etc. His crowning achievement was when a pupil bought in his father's horse (his dad was the local rag-man) leaving Dad with the cart at the school gates. Even better, and to my eyes the icing on the cake, the head teacher of the school was somehow coaxed into riding the horse twice round the school yard. Perhaps it was a dream fulfilled for the head; all I know is that John gained an excellent grade on leaving the school and he returned to his college studies with a story that kept him in drinks at the college bar for a long time.

Certainly all the college preparation, all the lectures, tutorials, expert advice took on a different perspective when you crossed the college–school divide. I do not wish to sound churlish or unkind but I learned more in my first term in the first school to which I was appointed after I graduated than in the whole of my college course.

So, the real world of teaching beckoned and here I was in a position to advise, nurture, protect and educate college students within my own class–teacher situation. What an awesome responsibility and, though it was some years before I was given a student to work with, the experience was, to say the least, interesting.

Over the years I have played classroom host to the occasional 'struggler', but the majority have been as well prepared as possible and more than able to manage. Some have been exceptionally gifted, with tremendous potential, and shown a special rapport with the children – boy, was I envious!

One of these was a young lady who brought a large container of lively cockroaches into the classroom, which was the focus of some splendid work. Sadly, a number of these creepy crawlies escaped and a frantic session was spent rounding them up. Thankfully the student was daring enough to handle these creatures, whilst for my part I observed and moved furniture but withdrew rather sharply when the catching had to be done.

Of course there are always the dramatic types, such as 'athletic' Bob, a great guy who happened to be with me during a swimming lesson. On seeing a little ten-year-old boy splashing about and appearing to be in difficulties, the brave student, sensing his moment of glory, flung himself spectacularly into the pool to rescue the pupil. Fortunately for him, the child avoided the would-be hero and swam off towards the shallow end. Brave Bob the rescuer, who was fully clothed, was left up to his armpits with billowing shirt, soggy tie, squelching PE shoes and a watch that didn't take to being submerged.

One thing is for sure, no matter how many years you work with children, be it on teaching practice as a student or as a learned and experienced teacher, there will be surprises all the way. Some days will be relatively ordinary – there will be highs and lows, laughter and tears, joy and despair – but no two days will ever be the same. And you will learn far more from your pupils than they will ever learn from you.

2

First School

'Do sit down.'
I did so and looked across the table at the man who was to be my first boss, the nicest man I ever worked with –'with' being the key word. You never worked for him but with him, together in partnership. That was the impression he gave and the reality when you actually worked in the school.

For those old enough to remember, he was a typical Alastair Sym look-alike, balding and with a calm, friendly appearance, almost like a granddad. He may not have had all the jargon that many of the so-called 'progressive' heads of the time spouted but he could, as I discovered over the years, have taught many of them much more about being a head teacher than they would care to admit.

Mr Clark was the head of a junior school and was interviewing various fresh-faced, fresh-out-of-college probationary teachers. It was my good fortune that he seemed to think I would be okay so we shook hands, I signed some papers and was invited to start the following Monday, three weeks before the beginning of the summer holidays in 1966.

Still wearing my L-plates, I had three weeks in July at my first school to sit in with various proper teachers. What an experience, what an education! I was introduced to Mrs G., the deputy head, a large kindly lady with heaving bosoms and a heaving class of more than forty fourth-year junior children, the 11+ plus scholars, the 'top' class. Entering the room, I noticed Mrs G. seated at an elevated desk, facing four rows of traditional lift-up seat, lift-up lid double desks. The children sat quietly, arms folded, in a tranquil classroom. This image has always stayed with me; in those moments when I was scurrying around the classroom, trying to do a hundred-and-one things all at once, I often yearned for this serene scenario!

Order and regularity were the watchwords. Children went about their business without fuss. There was no wandering around (there wasn't much room, even if they'd been allowed to); they were there to work, not talk, discuss, give too many opinions but get on with what they were told to do. It worked; the children knew what was expected, knew the order of things, felt safe, secure and stable. There was no need for locks on doors, behaviour programmes and star charts; none of these seemed to be required. Such things were not needed to clutter and congest the work of the teacher and class in a world that's disappeared – for better or for worse.

My most vivid memory was the Thursday art lesson. For the only time during the week, desks were moved to face each other front on; newspapers were used to cover the desks and the shiny glass Shipman paste jars were filled with water ready for the painting lesson. This routine went ahead every week on a Thursday, no matter what. If World War III had begun, if the Queen had made a visit, no matter – on a Thursday newspapers were on the desks and paste jars (small, squat, ribbed-glass jars only) were at the ready.

In time I visited them all – Mr T., Mrs C., Mrs L., Miss C.… wonderful teachers, indeed they were. Oh yes, by today's standard very old-fashioned, traditional, almost laughable, but they were respected, loved by the children they taught – well, most of them! No, I'm being unfair, these teachers were loved, though few children would admit it or even realise these feelings. They were 'real' teachers; they had an awe-inspiring quality.

You didn't see these people outside at the weekends, in shops, walking down the street, buying fish and chips or mixing with ordinary folk. Where did they go after school? It seemed as if at 4pm they faded away like the ink from Mrs G.'s inkwells faded into the thick white blotting paper; they just disappeared into school cupboards or locked themselves into the staffroom, only to re-appear at bell time the following morning!

Holiday time came, the big six weeks, the golden carrot of teaching, and soon it was September and time for me to step out on my own. Could I match these senior colleagues? Would I be out of my depth in the class, in the staffroom, in this strange insular school world? But hark, there's the old school bell! My first class, 3C, was ready for me, forty-eight, third-year junior pupils aged nine to ten. Here the serious learning was to begin… and I suppose that included the children too! This was where the rubber was to hit the road.

So, first morning, a bright September and Fred wouldn't listen. He wouldn't sit down, he wouldn't behave – in fact, he wouldn't anything. He just lounged in the far corner refusing to do, say or move. Help!

Just by chance (I think not!), the head was walking by outside my classroom in one of two prefabricated units detached from the main brick building – I wonder why they put me there? He knew the score and he knew Freddy. A brief nod through the window and he strode into my room. 'I just need to speak to Frederick for a moment… do excuse me.'

Grasping Fred firmly by the hand, they moved out and away towards the main building. One down, only forty-seven to go!

Fred returned later that morning, subdued and reluctantly ready to work.

*

During my first probationary year, I was fortunate to have another life-saver colleague stationed next door to me – Mrs L. or June. She was so much younger than the rest of the staff that I found it comforting that I could be on first-name terms with her.

On reflection it is quite funny that after two terms in the school one of the more senior men, whom I always addressed as Mr Thompson (known by the pupils as 'Tomboy'), spoke to me in the staffroom one morning. 'Bryan, I think you can call me Victor now.' An honour indeed! I suppose it made me feel that I was beginning to be accepted and part of the team.

So back to June, in the classroom next door. She was wonderful, my schoolteacher crush. How was it that she coped so well? She knew everything there was to know about the school – and there was such a lot to know. Fortunately, she was blessed with an abundance of patience and put up with the rookie next door. Many years later I was able to pay her back for her care and understanding by saving her school from serious flooding by an act of bravery and sheer foolishness... but that's a long, long story. Perhaps in another book!

You never forget the characters in your first class, even if you try! Although it seems a million years ago, will I ever forget Nosha, a tiny little boy who left such a huge impression? Poor Norman (his real name) struggled with everything – his sums, reading, talking, writing, etc. I'm convinced Nosha was born at the bottom of a slide and found it an uphill struggle from that point on. Yet he was a lovely boy and I thought he was great.

I can picture him: his black duffle coat, with only one wooden toggle left with which to fasten it up; a green wool roll-neck jumper, and a little screwed-up, puzzled face. Nosha would still be my number-one model for a *Beano* comic character from the Bash Street Gang.

The most wonderful revelation he ever made was when he told me about his dog. 'Sir, I've got an alstation' – yes, in Nosha speak, that's how it was pronounced – 'and it's just had pups.'

'How nice, Norman.'

'Yeah. I was in bed and I put my foot down and it was all wet and sticky. Our dog had had pups.'

It's not the sort of thing pupils tell you every day about their pets but that was Norman, always full of surprises. He often mentioned his dog, though it never seemed to have a name; it was always 'our dog' or 'the Alsatian' (sorry, that should be 'Alstation'!)

On Saturdays, or after school in the summer term, I often took a group of four or five children to visit local places of interest; those were the days when you weren't committed to endless after-school meetings. Yes, you actually had time to devote to pupils if you so wished – and

I so wished. Indeed, some of the meetings weren't needed in those days because so many teachers were solving, in practical ways, the problems that the meetings would have been considering. For instance, behavioural issues, motivation, building good relationships with children...

It was on one of these outings that I recall taking six of my first class (Nosha included) to the Transporter Bridge in Middlesbrough... no, I wasn't that desperate to get rid of them! We gasped for breath as we climbed the endless flight of steps to the top, and even more so at the view. We linked arms and walked across the wide metal planking at the top of the structure that joined the two giant towers either side of the bridge. It was absolutely magnificent; on the clearest of mornings the whole of Teesside, further inland and beyond past the coast, was at our feet. It was a wonderful shared experience but it would be impossible to do now, of course. Not only is access denied to the general public but, quite rightly in the present day and age, there is no way teachers would put their heads in the health-and-safety noose. And these days the documentation involved would be more strenuous to deal with than any planned activity!

*

Teachers were strict but, on occasions, there would be moments of madness. Wednesday afternoons were rather special, with all the children escorted to the hall, the curtains drawn, the projector wheeled in and a two-hour film show presented. They were educational films, of course, except for at Christmas time. One such film was called *The Grains Are Great Food*, a veritable classic of black and white (a mucky grey really), of epic proportions! Yawn, yawn... I must have seen this film at least a dozen times.

Where have these trade films gone? They were black-and-white films of such riveting and breathtakingly BORING subjects – surely they have been consigned to the bin! But hold on; these were the days of limited TV programmes, no videos, no CDs and no computers in schools, so we must guard against feeling scornful. In truth, the Wednesday film show was invaluable.

The big treat for staff was a break from the classroom routine. We were allowed to sit on the back row. I was seated ready for my first film show, note-pad and pencil in hand, ready to take my follow-up notes – not everything I had learned in college had been wasted.

There was a nudge against my arm and, in the semi-darkness of the hall, I heard the whispered words, 'Take three and pass it on.'

Suddenly I had a huge carrier-size bag deposited on my lap, crammed full of sweets. During the course of the afternoon the bag travelled back and forth along the back row. I thought it was such an hilarious and enjoyable ritual, especially as the sweets were taken and unwrapped so surreptitiously yet at the same time with ceremony and aplomb, befitting the assembled gathering of 'Sirs' and 'Misses' of this great educational establishment.

The children seemed to pay no attention to this quaint practice and before long I absorbed this delightful tradition in my weekly work pattern until it became second nature. Of course it was rather a financial drain, especially to a young teacher, when it was your turn to provide the goodies for the week. Only the very best-quality confectionary was allowed, none of your 'pick-and-mix' stuff. I must confess that I was often tempted to throw in a few disgusting, ill-flavoured items or place something like a set of plastic false teeth inside the bag. However, the thought of disturbing the weekly programme made me decide against it; besides, had I been rumbled such behaviour would have been worthy of instant dismissal.

There was an unforgettable occasion when the Wednesday goody-bag ritual was interrupted. Mr T., our long-standing projectionist, was in the middle of changing reels, a most complicated feat of engineering, and we were awaiting reel number two of a black-and-white film about India. Somehow the leading edge of the film had not taken up through the gate and the thin filmstrip pushed open the side panel and was snaked about in great curved loops on the floor. Mr T. was attending to a less-than-enthusiastic filmgoer in front of his machine and was temporarily distracted. The rest of us, from what I recall, were discussing our work programmes and how the film could be used effectively – or maybe we were just gossiping. Suddenly our attention was drawn to this mass of writhing, cellulose ribbon bubbling about on the floor, increasing by a fantastic rate of footage as each second passed by.

Eventually the lights were switched on and the machine unplugged as the monster slithered about in a huge shimmering mass on the floor. Having stumbled over one or two half-blinking children, Mr T. wrapped his arms around the great pile of film, wrestled his way through the back doors and deposited the heap in the entrance hall. A member of staff kept some semblance of order in the hall as the rest of us performed a too-many-cooks' exercise with the blob. At length (an ideal choice of word!) we had the film strung out; it must have been over sixty metres long and stretched along the outside corridor into the playground. Staff picked feverishly at little clumps of knotted film. I gave up on my ravelled piece after ten minutes or so; as our frustration grew, we realised that the children's knowledge of India that afternoon would be limited to reel one only.

My abiding memory of the afternoon is of Mr T. scooping great armfuls of film into a large cardboard paper-towel box and muttering one or two well-chosen phrases. What became of the film I never knew and never asked. As they would say nowadays, don't go there – and as far as I know, no one did. The disaster was never mentioned again – well, not within earshot of Mr T.!

Of course, in my first year my class was very special and together we learned our way through the term. They needed patience as I painstakingly moved from week to week with all the enthusiasm, energy and foolhardiness of a young probationary teacher. What I lacked in experience and expertise (in abundance compared to colleagues around me, so it seemed) I tried to make up for in effort and enterprise, which was often very ill-considered. Each day was crammed with incident as I readily responded to all the youngsters in my charge.

*

There was the day one pupil brought in a toy gun belt and two plastic six-shooters from his cowboy set at home. Here was an opportunity not to be missed. Towards the end of a maths lesson, just before milk-bottle time, I strapped on my hardware (the toy gun belt, that is – no computers in those days!), which was on teacher's desk for safety, and strolled in front of the class as the sum books were being collected.

'Hey, *hombre*, go for your gun!' In true Western fashion, I drew my guns, spun round and pointed the weapons at the door – a door that had opened just a split second earlier by the head teacher! What an embarrassment!

He was an even better actor than me and, without a trace of emotion, he continued, 'Good morning, Class 4.' He lowered his glasses and peered over them. 'Good morning... Mr Cross.'

As he shut the door and gracefully retreated, I'm sure with the hint of a smile, my class erupted with laughter. They were getting used to 'Sir's' strange ways. I didn't continue the charade but quickly returned the guns to the holsters. The 'Red-Faced Kid' moseyed over to his desk, laid down his gun belt and gave out the milk straws. Some days later I was equally red faced in the staffroom when the head, during an informal discussion on the merits of television in the home, quite wickedly found opportunity to comment, 'Mr Cross, you rather like cowboy films, don't you?'

My encouragement for freedom of expression knew no bounds. One Friday afternoon, when the timetable of school lessons was slightly relaxed, I decided not to read a story, have a quiz or instigate some light-hearted class debate; no, I would give the children the floor. It developed into a free-expression period – tell us about your hobbies or interests, sing a song, do a dance. Indeed, it was a latter-day *Britain's Got Talent*.

'Please, sir, can I tell a joke?' asked Jane.

Now Jane was a quiet, pleasant little girl – why not let her tell a joke? It would be good for her self-confidence and development. Big mistake!

But I fell for it and, seated at the back of the class, I felt good as Jane, smartly dressed and coming from one of the better parts of our school catchment area, took centre stage at the front of the class. I bet other teachers haven't been able to develop this initiative from this shy, rather withdrawn child, I thought smugly to myself. I was about to be surprised!

'So this little boy went to the doctor's,' Jane began. 'And the doctor says to him, what's wrong?' (So far okay.)

'"Well, every time I go for a wee there's crumbs in the toilet."' Jane put her head down as she said this. Where's this leading, I wondered.

'"Crumbs," said the doctor.

'"Yes," replied the little boy.

'"Let's get this right," the doctor said. "Every time you go to the toilet there's crumbs?"'

Jane's telling this story really well, I thought, but get on with it. The class are starting to giggle. Have they heard this one before? Should I stop her?

She continued. '"I know what's wrong with you," said the doctor. "You're pi**ing crackers!"'

Well, the class fell apart with laughter for a few seconds then stopped and, as one, slowly turned around for my reaction.

'Thank you, Jane. It was a bit rude, wasn't it?' I said.

'Please, sir, can I tell one?' called out a voice.

'No! No! No!' I called back. 'Terry, you certainly can't!'

I was catching on fast.

*

What a collection of characters there seemed to be. One boy was nicknamed 'Free-Frees'; apparently this came about because he couldn't pronounce his 'ths'. This was highlighted one fateful day some years earlier when he struggled to recite his 'free' (sorry, three) times table. He got stuck on the bit where 'free' of the 'frees' made nine and he had been asked by the teacher to repeat it 'free' times, would you believe!

Then there was the tiny girl, who regularly came to school wearing the same scruffy clothes, so it appeared. Feeling very charitable and do-goodish, I zoomed around my family collecting a bundle of good-quality, clean, second-hand clothes. A few days later this sack of clothes went home with the child but, sadly, she returned wearing the same clothing as before. Certainly she never wore her new 'wardrobe' to school; whether her mum kept them for best I will never know. Sceptics or realists on the staff had their own theories and told me them, some quite forcefully. Perhaps my 'what a wonderful kind chap you are' ideas floundered early in my career, but it was a lesson to be learned that you need to be very sensitive in doing this sort of thing. It needs to be handled far better than my bull-in-a-china-shop, ham-fisted efforts.

*

A few weeks into the school year and it was the turn of 'my' class to 'do' the class assembly for that particular week as each class took turns on a weekly rota. As it was the Harvest Festival season, I decided that would be the theme. Enter Geoffrey! Now Geoff was very tall and even more noticeable was his bright mop of ginger hair. A veritable Belisha beacon, he was about to give a most unforgettable Harvest Festival performance.

Undoubtedly the tallest boy in the class, if not the school, Geoff was difficult to place in a class group. Where should I position him on the school stage for our whole-class assembly? Right in the middle of the middle row sitting on a PE bench, with a row behind him standing and a row in front, sitting cross-legged? There was nowhere else for him, really; how could I possibly balance him up with anyone or anything – perhaps it was an open sack of carrots at one end of the line and Geoff at the other!

All of the class had a part to play and Geoffrey was no different. So far everything had been okay during practices; a few dropped lines, along with one or two apples suffering a similar fate and a slightly bruised marrow, but otherwise not too bad. When the day of the performance arrived, I was quite apprehensive with all the school in the hall but nothing ventured... and off we went. 'Today Class 4 would like to tell you about harvest time...'

About halfway through it was Geoff's turn. Lifting a huge, golden-brown, crusty loaf in both hands he was supposed to say:

'Bread is a lovely thing to eat.

God bless the barley and the wheat.'

It was simple but what he had to say and what he actually said did not go to plan.

'Bread is a lovely...' Silence!

He lowered the loaf onto his lap then, after a few seconds, lifted it up again.

'Bread is a lovely...' Silence!

Slipping from my chair at the front side of the hall, and semi-screened by the piano, I whispered the prompt: 'Bread is a lovely thing... THING.'

Geoffrey raised the bread again.

'Bread is a lovely thing...' There was silence again!

Once more I whispered out, 'God bless.'

Again he tried. 'Bread is a lovely thing, God bless...' Silence!

Oh no! In my panic I'd fed him the wrong line, now *I'd* got it wrong! I whispered the line as it should be yet again:

'Bread is a lovely thing to eat.

'God bless the…' Surely this would be enough to get him through.

He raised the loaf again.

'Bread is a lovely thing to eat,

'God bless the…' Silence.

All the class knew Geoffrey's words; some were whispering, hands in front of their mouths, some were muttering, 'Go on, Geoffrey!' The girl who was to speak next just sat there, clutching a big bag of flour. Why didn't she start? Speak! Say something!

By now it was getting farcical and some pupils in the vast congregation were trying, unsuccessfully, to suppress their laughter and shuffling on the floor. Everyone focussed on Geoff. He kept lifting the huge crusty loaf up and down, as though he were working out in the gym.

As all the class knew Geoffrey's words – in fact everyone knew everyone else's words because we had practised long and hard – I decided to resign myself to standing up from a crouching position behind the piano. Speaking to them in a sort of 'I give up' voice, I said, 'All say it.' They did.

'Bread is a lovely thing to eat

God bless the barley and the wheat.'

Geoffrey beamed a great smile out of sheer relief as he held above his head the brown, crusty loaf that gleamed in the autumn sunshine. It was very much in the style of an FA Cup winning captain. As Geoffrey lifted the 'trophy', guess what? It was something I've never experienced since, in more than forty years of teaching: the whole school applauded spontaneously!

It's true!

*

Of course, things concerning pupils also happened out of school. I can recall one grey Saturday afternoon, just after watching Middlesbrough Football Club being defeated at Ayresome Park (no change there, then!), driving my dad's car through Stockton, near the Parish Church. It was raining, the Boro had been beaten, Dad was not feeling too well and the mood in the car was not too pleasant when, as I moved down the inside lane, a car from a side junction near the library collided with us.

Dad's car was his pride and joy and I was only driving because he was feeling poorly, so with all the other events of the afternoon he was not in the best of spirits. Leaping out of the car and forgetting he was ill, he went hysterical, screaming and shouting at the lady motorist, who clearly was in the wrong and even more clearly had bashed into the side of our car.

As I got out of the car to inspect the damage and calm Dad, two small heads popped out of the back window of the offending vehicle. 'Hello, sir, are you alright?'

They were two children from school; one of the girls was actually a pupil in my class. They gave me a cheery greeting with all the innocence and naivety of children. Didn't they realise they were involved in the most serious road traffic accident occurring in Teesside that year – well, according to my dad it was!

'Oh well,' I thought, 'there's one less member for our Parent-Teachers' Association!'

3

1966 – And All That!

'THEY THINK IT'S ALL OVER... IT'S ONLY JUST BEGINNING!!'

(World Cup commentary)

And what a platform of enthusiasm, drive and motiva-tion for a young, mad-about-sport teacher about to prepare his first football team. Well, of course it's about football – football in school. England had just lifted the World Cup; Geoff Hurst had banged in his hat trick; 'Giraffe' Jack Charlton had carried the emotion of the nation, while his brother Bob was just superb. Nobby Stiles had danced his jig and yours truly was sitting down with the most ragged set of football strips you could imagine. Wow, did I need some inspiration from the England team!

The strips were handed to me in a big dusty cardboard box. The first thing I noticed in there was a sheet with the last two seasons' results. We had lost every game; 1–0 against was the highlight of last season, or maybe it was occasion when we scored two goals – although to be fair the opposition scored seven!

So here was the kit: mucky-yellow shirts with a white V-neck collar, most of which were threadbare. The white shorts, with thick elastic around the waist, were huge and when wet must have acted like a sponge and doubled in weight! Finally the socks, oh the socks – only seven of them, yellowish with white tops, each with a texture of cardboard and able to stand up on its own. The final pieces of equipment I inherited were a canvas bag containing a leather football with bladder and laces, a large hook-like instrument, an even longer blunt needle for threading and lacing up the football, plus a giant tin of Wrens Yellow Dubbin. Sir Alf Ramsey, World Cup winning manager, you wouldn't have known where to start!

Our pitch was the Rec and the goalposts had to be carried about 300 yards from the school to the ground. Professional players talk about pre-match preparation – they would have loved mine…

Arrive at school 9am, Saturday; wrestle for forty-five minutes pushing the bladder into the leather case of the ball; string up the bladder tube after inflating the bladder; lace up the football and slap some dubbin on. Spend at least half an hour fine-tuning the pitch, i.e. removing bricks, glass bottles, pram wheels and last night's fish-and-chip papers. Landfill the goalmouth areas with sawdust and fill in the line markings with the same, where necessary.

Return to school to appease the caretaker; no those children on the roof aren't on my team. None of our players have that sort of balance! Pity! 'Hey, son, are you from this school? Get down! No, don't run away. Fancy a game of football?'

By now, the early arrivals have come in. These are the fringe players, eager to help with the goalposts. Dodging the local bread van and milk float, the posts are safely carried across the road ready for erection, not an easy task considering the uprights had to be dropped into sockets on the field. These metal sockets, permanently sunk into the grass, were often filled with a varied assortment of objects. It took me twenty minutes one morning to remove an old tennis ball – and sometimes they contained liquid!

Then we all get changed, we have the team talk and we play the game. Phew!

Truth to tell, I loved it and was probably far more enthusiastic than any of the players. My commitment was such that I wore a tracksuit and even showed my legs by wearing shorts in decent weather. This was a far cry from a number of less-keen colleagues who refereed games in a remarkable array of costumes – flannel blazers, raincoats, duffle coats, etc. I fondly recall one who took to the field regularly wearing wellies, a long mackintosh, flat cap and holding a rolled umbrella that he used on two occasions, if memory serves me rightly, in a drizzly period during a game. This ref, whose name or school I will not mention, often turned his back to the play, lit a cigarette and continued to puff his way through many a fixture.

Positional play was not an outstanding feature of these less than enthusiastic refs; many would take up a position on the centre line at a mid-point between the centre spot and the touchline, pivoting as the play moved back and forth. Players and parents never challenged decisions, thank goodness. In those days, the teacher's word was law. Goal-line technology – forget it!

*

Then came the big day, a bright and sunny Saturday in September with my team ready for the first match. I had prepared them well, with a practice every lunchtime, and we were eagerly awaiting the game.

Having gone through all the preliminaries, we strode on to the pitch in our less-than-pristine strips. Our opponents from a big school, with a fearsome reputation on the pitch, had arranged to meet us at the ground. At 10.15, as we moved on to the pitch for a warm-up, I noticed a minibus pull up at the far end of the Rec. Out stepped the Roseworth School team; sporting brand-new red tracksuits, they sprinted across towards us, like wolves approaching a flock of lambs. Staring open-mouthed, our team was rooted to the spot. I was rather taken aback too, only to be stirred by one of my players. 'They look posh, don't they, sir?'

Oh, they looked posh alright. Underneath the tracksuits were new red football strips. 'What a waste of money! Why can't they spend it on books, pencils and other essential equipment?' whispered an evil, envious voice inside me.

'Gift from our Parents' Association,' beamed their proud teacher/manager. 'Ever so generous, don't you think?'

'Oh yeah,' I replied and was tempted to ask what he was doing with their cast-off kit.

We were trailing 1–0 within the first five of the twenty-five minutes each way game, a narrow margin partly due to both teams being distracted by the new strips. The opposition were preening themselves; we were admiring them jealously. Perhaps this was the reason why we were playing as though we were in a playground kick-and-rush game. Slowly, however, some of the basic things I had mentioned were sinking in.

Although I was refereeing and unable to coach, I could question some of my team as they passed me by: 'Should you be on this side of the pitch?' or 'Are you playing centre-forward today?'

At half time there was a five-minute team talk and then, on the resumption of the match and completely against the run of play, we managed to score an equalising goal. As the ball crossed the goal line, my team could hardly believe it. Neither could I.

'Yes, you've scored! We have a goal! Go back to your half, ready for the re-start,' I said to my team, who were in a dream.

They did and, in spite of a few scares late on, we managed to hold on for a draw. Well, the Reds didn't sprint off quickly to their minibus after the game.

Having exchanged pleasantries with their teacher, I gathered together the heroes of our school and praised them for their efforts. I guaranteed it was a weekend they would remember for some time. We got a point! We drew with Roseworth!

As we carted back the goalposts, there was great noise and excitement. Whirling players hurtled back to school, with passers-by hastily avoiding goalposts, swinging boots and corner flags.

Alas, this was our high point of the season and it turned out to be our only point gained in ten fixtures. But we enjoyed our football and in the following years we improved tremendously and produced some excellent footballers, one of whom gained domestic, European and international honours on the football field. We enjoyed good parental support and shared many happy memories.

One of the finest players happened to be a girl – yes, I know it's different now, but remember this was the 1960s – called Dawn. A girl who pestered me to play with such determination that, in the end, I had to give her a chance. I'm glad I did. She was superb and would be in my top ten players if I were compiling a list of the best primary-school players I have worked with in more than thirty years of school football. It would be quite a long list too, with at least two of my players becoming successful professional footballers. Not only was Dawn in my team but also in my third-year junior class, so I can happily say she was a wonderful pupil and a joy to teach.

Dawn played regularly for the school team; she was a striker even before the days when they were called strikers. She scored some great goals and became quite a star. Her mum and dad were lovely too and were regular touchline supporters. News seemed to travel about this girl footballer and, within quite a short space of time, local and national newspapers became interested. Perhaps foolishly in retrospect, the school allowed photos to be taken and articles written. Then came the TV!

I recall it well. I was sitting at home on a Tuesday afternoon during a half-term holiday, when there was a knock on the door. Who should be standing there but the familiar face of a Tyne-Tees TV presenter; her name escapes me now but she had a distinctive Canadian accent and appeared regularly on the Tyne-Tees news magazine programme. She wanted to do a piece about our girl footballer. Typical of the media, who don't observe school half-terms, they couldn't accept that it was difficult as the school was closed. The woman was as persuasive as a TV celebrity can be and cajoled me into setting up an interview immediately. I arranged to meet her and the film crew within the hour on the school field (we had since left the Rec and had our own pitch adjacent to the school) so it was time to get moving.

Where to begin? Why did I let myself be talked into this? First I had to track down Dawn. Thankfully, she was near her home, playing football. What else?

'Hi Dawn,' went the conversation.

'Hi Mr C.'

'Dawn, how would you like to appear on TV?' You know, the sort of everyday exchange between a teacher and a pupil!

To cut a long story short, I erected a set of posts on the field and wandered around the streets near the school knocking on doors and rousing as many players/school pupils as possible.

'But, sir, I'm not in the team. I can't play football!'

'That doesn't matter. Get down to the school field, we're on the telly.'

Eventually the TV cameras rolled. Dawn was seen in action, shooting a goal, heading a ball and dribbling between numerous other players. She was interviewed and so was I. Standing there like a latter-day *Match of the Day* manager I was able to get in all the clichés: 'over the moon', 'game of two halves', etc., etc. Well, I wasn't going to miss out on this big-time opportunity.

I enjoyed the feast but then came the famine a few days later, in the form of a letter. Remember we are talking about the late 1960s, liberated in many swinging ways but not on the football fields of England. The English Schools' Football Association letter forcefully pointed out, with many 'respectfullys' and 'you will appreciates', that girls should and could not be allowed to play football in a boys' team, even at primary-school level. Did they think we segregated boys and girls within our P.E and games lessons?

What a bombshell. Dawn was one of our best players; how were we going to manage? How would her parents react? But more importantly by far, how would she take it? It was so difficult to break the news to her and a very sad thing for me to do. She was a young child and, as you can imagine, there were a lot of tears and upset but the directive from the ESFA was quite clear.

However, competitive games against other schools were played on a friendly basis (not that children are able to distinguish between 'friendly' and 'competitive') even though the results would not stand in terms of the league and cup. How ridiculous!

Before each game, I explained the situation to the opposing school team. Apart from one or two who objected 'Well, rules are rules and we don't want to get into bother with the ESFA', we managed to have Dawn play in a number of matches against other schools, even though we were not fully obeying the directive. On quite a few occasions, having conceded goals from the boot of this girl player, I'm sure many schools thought they should have enforced the ban and maybe then they would have won!

Later Dawn went on to gain honours in various sports, representing her country and travelling abroad. You tend to lose track of pupils over the years but I do believe at one time she was teaching in a Northumberland school. Teaching – PE!

*

During the time of Dawn's exploits on the soccer field, I was hounded and pestered by a little blond-haired boy who always seemed to be kicking a football near the edge of the pitch whether it was a practice game or a school versus school game.

'Can I play for your football team?'

'Do you go to this school, son?'

'No, I'm in the infants, but my sister Karen does.'

'That's good. What's your name?'

'Gary.'

'Well, Gary with a sister in our juniors, what's your second name?'

'Pallister, I'm Gary Pallister.'

The difficulty was that he was only in the infant department and infant children didn't play in junior-school teams. I certainly didn't want another letter from the ESFA! Gary was big enough, keen enough and, as it proved, more than good enough to play but I had to say no.

In time he moved up to the juniors and eventually played in the school team. I have to admit that even before he moved up he often joined in our practices. There was no fear of him being hurt or made to feel not good enough. Quite the reverse!

He was in a superb eleven-a-side team of Year 4 (second-year juniors) players. What a team: even as young as nine to ten years of age they were excellent, showing tremendous potential. Sadly, in terms of the football, I left for promotion to deputy head teacher at the end of their Year 4 and was unable to coach them for the final two years in school. Four boys in particular were outstanding: Gary Popple ('Popeye'); Antony Ford; Andy Morris, and Gary Pallister ('Pally'). I wonder what became of them?

A game I remember vividly was against St Mark's School, I played our Year 4 team, though our opponents were in Year 6 and a lot older. In spite of this we won the game, which was at St Mark's School, and played superbly. 'Pally' impressed in particular, carrying the ball upfield from defence into attack with his long, striding action. Little did I realise that in a few years time he would be repeating the process for Middlesbrough Football Club, Manchester United and England.

And let's not forget big sister, Karen, school and town high-jump champion in her final year at school. Being of similar height to Gary, I remember joking with her at the town finals, 'Karen, you've no problem here. Most of your body is above the bar before you jump!' She was a lovely girl and seemed to get in far less bother than her little brother in school. It's alright, Gary, I won't tell!

They were both fortunate in having very supportive parents. Indeed, such was their support and encouragement, if I could have used Gary's mam and dad (along with so many others I can recall) to act as football foster parents then maybe over the years there would have been more than one playing for a top premiership team! This is not a criticism of the parents of many of the soccer-mad boys but praise for the ones who turned up to encourage and support them. Gary was fortunate in many respects and I am so proud for him and his family. On the other side of the coin, how sad it has been over the years to see youngsters with equal potential somehow throw it all away due to lack of parental guidance or sheer disinterest.

*

Though I have some wonderful memories of school football, not all were jolly good fun – and I am not talking about being beaten. Defeats, and how you handle them with the children, can have as many benefits as victories. It's about knowing how to win in the right way.

No, I'm thinking of the time at the end of a school fixture when I went into the stock room adjoining my classroom to get changed and discovered about 80p of loose change missing from my trouser pockets. I hoped against hope that it had fallen out whilst I was getting ready to referee the match but, although I had a good search on the floor, I feared it had been taken.

The following day, I heard rumours in class that one of the boys had been buying lots of sweets at the corner shop after the game. I suspected then what had happened.

At break-time the boy concerned, who had been sent for from another class, came into my room. I hoped he had a good excuse; I hoped there was some simple explanation because I didn't want him to have taken the money. In he came. I didn't say anything, I just looked up at him from my desk. He lowered his head and started to cry. I never mentioned the missing money; maybe I should have done. All I talked about was trust and how disappointing it is when trust between two people disappears. I was upset, perhaps selfishly thinking I had such a wonderful rapport with the team that they wouldn't dream of doing anything underhand to the ever-popular, dashing young sports teacher.

Of course I forgave the lad for what had happened, though he had to be reprimanded; for the benefit of the rest of the team he had to be *seen* to be reprimanded. I was sure that many of the other players who didn't know would find out eventually. He missed three games for the school and, as one of the regular players in the team, that was punishment enough. As far as I was concerned the matter was over and I hoped he had learned from his error. In future I always locked my changing cupboard; I still trusted the boys but I was determined not to put temptation in their way.

As the years went by, I moved on to other schools, running other football teams and happily winning cups and trophies. I was happy because it was reward for the efforts of the teams I worked with. I encouraged the players to play with fairness, good team spirit and the desire to win. In all my teams I advocated this desire to win and to be disappointed in defeat, but not to the extent of cheating or stopping at nothing to win. Accepting victory graciously and defeat honourably was important. In the realms of school sport, there is such a massive opportunity for children to learn life lessons that can be of tremendous value in preparing them for adulthood. It has always saddened me when adults, whether teachers, parents, or supporters of any kind, have said to children after a defeat, 'Oh it doesn't matter, it's just a game.'

I know exactly what they are trying to say but it sounds so patronising. Children should experience disappointment, otherwise the activity has less worth; it should be part of the growing-up process. Get a defeat in perspective and within a short period of time use the initial upset to focus on how things will be different next time and how mistakes can be used to build for the future.

I digress... So, I moved to other schools, as I mentioned earlier, and my regret is that the teams from my first school never had success in terms of winning things, though there were some outstanding players. In more than thirty years of school football at primary level, apart from a handful of players (Adam Boyd from HUFC and Paul Hutton, in particular) my best eleven team, plus subs, all came from my first school so long ago.

It is a popular pastime for football enthusiasts to compile a team of their favourite players over the years. The following team, at their best at primary-school age, would have been more than a match for any school: Antony Ford ('Fordy'); John Davison ('Davo'); Gary Pallister ('Pally'); Ian Marshall ('Masha'); John Kirton; Colin Wennington;

Mike Nelson; Gary Popple ('Popeye'); John Hart ('J-J');
Dawn Nicholson ('Nicko'); Ranjit Dastidar ('Rainbow').

Subs: Andy Morris; Andrew Boult 'Archie'; Pete Smith.

The time I spent with these and other children was
a privilege and we certainly clocked up the hours. At
least three sessions after school every week – and most of
the planned practices of thirty minutes would extend to
one-hour plus! In fact in more than fifty years as a soccer
enthusiast, having watched all the major games over these
years – World Cups, League Championships, European
games, etc. – I have seen few joys that surpass those of
young schoolboy footballers seeing their name on the
school team sheet and being given their school football
kit for the first time.

Before the final whistle blows on this chapter, my
abiding school football memory is sitting in the middle
of the school field during my first school year with the
rain drizzling down at half-time in a game we were losing
5–0. One of the boys, mud-spattered, wet hair plastered
down, looked at me with all the hope and expectancy of a
toddler on Santa's knee and said, 'We've still got a chance,
haven't we, sir?'

I can't recall what I said in reply but I know I gave him
a hug as I said it – and we lost 7–3! That was okay by me.

4

'H-H-H-Hartlepool'

Deputy head teacher sounds rather good, so bags packed off I went to deepest, darkest Hartlepool, a town in which I would work for more than twenty years. My new school was a junior school, a neat and tidy establishment. It had four rooms upstairs, four rooms downstairs (one of which was mine), which led in turn down a corridor past the library to the entrance hall, bounded on one side by the multi-purpose hall and on the other the head-teacher's room and general office. My room was nearest to the cloakrooms and shower room, positioned at the bottom of the stairs – a prime site for action over the years.

It was difficult getting to grips with a new staff, new organisation and especially a new class. Very smart, smartly uniformed and polite, the children were a joy to work with (most children are, believe it or not!), especially Robert in my Year 6 class who gave me the seal of approval on the Friday of my first week.

It was home time; the bell had gone and Robert was kneeling down near his table fastening his bag. Most of the class had left the room. 'Mr C.,' he said in a steady confident voice – Robert always had a steady confident voice – 'I think you'll be alright here!' It was comforting to know.

Robert, fortunately for me, was right. I was indeed alright there, due in the main to a great bloke J.K.W., the head teacher, and some splendid staff, teaching and non-teaching.

I was taken aback during the first week, however, when during a lunchtime I was shown some photographs of a coach dramatically enveloped in thick, black smoke, windows shattered and thoroughly burnt out. These images were taken towards the end of a school visit the previous term, when the vehicle, a few miles away from school, suddenly burst into flames. The children and teachers all behaved heroically, escaping slightly shocked but in the main unharmed.

'Oh,' laughed one of the staff as he handed me the prints. 'That sort of thing's always happening at this school!'

Help, what have I let myself in for?

*

The first term was most eventful during my 'settling-in' period.

There was the morning I was disturbed by a flurry of children bursting into the school building before morning bell.

'Sir, there are cows in the yard!'

'Children, don't be silly. Let me see.'

On releasing the roller blind at the window in my room, which overlooked the playground, I saw to my dismay that the pupils were right. No less than thirty Friesian cattle were mooing and buffeting each other in the yard, outside all the ground-floor classroom windows.

Living in the countryside at the time, I summoned up my best farmer-type pose and tried to move some of the beasts onto the school field, assisted by a few members of staff not averse to a bit of bovine bovver.

Eventually the local farmer arrived and they were herded back to where they should have been (the cattle not the children!). Sadly, the smaller of the two playgrounds was out of bounds that day due to a series of plate-shaped deposits left by our Friesian friends.

Well, they'd had the fire, now the earthquake (thanks to our pounding four-legged beasties); we couldn't possibly have the flood… could we? Oh yes we could!

Again it was an early-morning experience; a cry from a tiny cupboard off the cloakroom area. I saw water seeping from under the door. Nothing ventured, I investigated. Have the cattle returned, I thought. No, not a bit of it: it was none other than one of our cleaning ladies, trying without success to push a water pipe, under pressure, back into a valve in one of our main water boilers. Soaked from head to foot, she struggled bravely to force the squirting pipe back into the boiler nozzle as gallons and gallons of water gushed out. After what seemed an eternity, we located the cut-off valve, stopped the flow and awaited the arrival of the maintenance engineers – but not before the cloakroom area was awash to a depth of about two to three inches. Once more staff, teaching and non-teaching, used mops, brushes and improvised with large rolls of paper towels to remedy a situation beyond the normal call of duty.

Shoes rather moist, the mopping-up brigade eventually shouldered arms at about ten o'clock while the grateful children had an extended and welcome pre-school playtime. Surprisingly few school materials were ruined and we made the best of the day. Certainly our gallant Mrs Mop sloshed her way home later that morning having performed her heroic 'finger in the dyke' deed, which had prevented serious water damage to the school.

Between these incidents, seriously good-quality teaching went on. As a young, enthusiastic staff, we had a very responsive school of children. Almost all staff volunteered to take lunchtime or after-school activities: sport, art, music and dance were the main ones but there were other clubs and societies, all of which were well attended.

The fact that we had a one hour and forty minutes lunch break gave us time to devote to these pursuits. Perhaps the reason so many staff and children participated was due to the lengthy break; after all, a hundred minutes can be a long time without any structured programme. In addition, the teachers were keen to develop their particular interests. For the first three or four years I was there, things were really buzzing – and one day in particular we created our own buzz!

I was on playground duty with another young male teacher when we happened to see one of the pupils flying a kite. Joining in the fun, my colleague and I had a go, zooming the stunt kite in huge spirals above the school field.

'You must be practising for next week,' we joked. 'It's National Kite Week!'

Playtime ended but the following day several more kites appeared. There was no cause for alarm as the children were enjoying themselves. Then came the phone call from the local newspaper: 'We understand it's National Kite Week next week. Can we come down and do an article for the paper?'

I can't recollect who took the phone call but the press-man must have been very persuasive. He had made his mind up to get a story no matter what; it must have been a quiet week for news!

Well, blow (pardon the pun), he could have one.

Photos were taken, words were written and the following week we celebrated National Kite Week! The fact that no one else in the nation was flying kites that week didn't matter as far as we were concerned: it was our National Kite Week. Perhaps we should have informed more people! Oddly enough, following our newspaper appearance, one or two local head teachers rang to enquire about the activity and, with rather red faces, we had to admit that National Kite Week, however stimulating and educational, was totally self-generated!

I thought at one point of informing the newspaper of the spoof. Perhaps the headline would have been *Flights of Fancy*. No, maybe it was not a good idea. Matter closed and put to bed as quickly as possible – and no more joking with children in the yard. Shows how rumours can develop.

*

My time at the school was packed with incident; things happened, with highs and lows, and during my thirteen years (surely the number tells it all) at the school I saw many changes. Head teachers, staff – both teaching and non-teaching – and on a personal and domestic front, there was a most distressing period in my life when things seemed to hit rock bottom. Although it is not really a subject for this book, it is worth mentioning that during the most difficult year of my life I was supported by the very best class of children I could have wished for, in addition to a wonderful school staff. The context of this book is, of course, school but, had it not been for my family and Christian faith, my school career would most likely have ended at that point.

As I'm sure you will have gathered, football was again prominent in my school life, in spite of my additional managerial responsibilities. I ran the school second eleven (the B team) and they were successful in winning various cups and trophies. Furthermore, I was able to pass on many of the younger boys to the A team where, with a little more polishing from an equally soccer-mad colleague, they went on to a bigger stage to win town and county honours. Perhaps it was the Lancashire/Yorkshire combination; our teams over those ten years or so always came up smelling of roses (red and white, of course). I doubt if many schools could equal our winning ways at primary level during the mid 1970s to late 1980s, certainly not in Cleveland.

Although this friend and colleague, a dyed-in-the-wool footballer (although sadly a Blackburn boy!) had plenty of skill with the leather ball, he had never played golf, so one day I thought I'd give him an introduction. I had a half set of clubs and, as a mature golfer with six months' experience, I decided to whet his appetite and extend his sporting horizons. I shouldn't have bothered. Will I ever forget the occasion? It was a once-in-a-lifetime experience, thank goodness.

We sauntered onto the school field just off the Tarmac yard. The whole length of the grass in front of us was at least 150 yards to the boundary fence and the South Fens housing estate beyond. My idea was to knock a few balls with my 'student' for about fifteen minutes until the first batch of children came out of the dining hall. In actual fact only one ball was struck – but what a strike!

I placed the gleaming white ball on the tee, selected a driving wood and handed it over to the novice. 'Just give it a good old whack.'

I can't remember how he 'addressed' the ball (I was well-versed in golf speak) and I'm pretty sure he can't; all I know is that he gave the club an almighty swing and the sound of club head on ball was like a rifle shot. The ball went rocketing off like an Exocet missile, soared upwards and away, over the distant fence, over the roofs of the semi-detached houses and continued to who knows where. I swear it was the most powerful golf drive I'd ever seen; had it been on a fairway, we would have been looking at a carry of more than 300 yards. Eat your heart out, Tiger Woods!

Beyond the estate stretched the Stockton to Hartlepool dual carriageway; whether the ball reached the main road or whether it ricocheted off houses in the estate I don't know. I do know we gathered up the remaining balls, irons and bag very quickly; it was time for an early lunch! Thankfully we never heard of anyone or anything damaged by this potentially lethal projectile, though we lived in fear and trembling for some days afterwards.

Having experienced the golf-ball drama in the spring term, I really should have known the risk I was taking during the following summer term. There was I, bowling on the cricket strip – a hessian mat in the middle of the school field – when the same teacher faced up to my devilishly cunning spin bowling during a lunchtime practice with pupils. He was beaten 'all ends up' for the first two balls before leaning on his back foot and, in cavalier fashion, crashing a sensational drive first bounce on the yard, which took out a huge classroom window. *My* classroom window! This man was dangerous; this man was one to whom I would never bowl again or place down a golf ball to be despatched. In Mr P.'s hands, even tiddlywinks would be fraught with danger!

*

Never a dull moment in this school, you may be thinking – how true. Sure, we had our bread-and-butter days but things always seemed to be happening, especially during my early days. The children were kept on their toes – no, I'm not referring to them having to dodge cricket balls! There was an industry about the place from a young, willing and dedicated staff led by a head who gave us the freedom to try out new ideas and initiatives. We, the children and staff, enjoyed being there and the place was alive. Certainly we knocked ourselves out for the children in the school – and one day I did that quite literally.

I'm sure the pupils, all thirty boys, recall the incident with some amusement. It started as they were putting the finishing touches to a squadron of Spitfires and Messerschmitts in a craft lesson. Yes, thanks once again to generous donations, we had hundreds of cardboard tubes from the inside of paper towels; armed with these, egg boxes and other scrap materials, our World War II planes were almost ready for painting and displaying as part of our history topic work.

Suddenly there was a message to report to the Luftwaffe Headquarters in Berlin – sorry, I do get carried away with these history projects! It was a message to go to the phone about a forthcoming football match. I sprinted down the corridor, answered the phone in seconds and returned, racing down the corridor.

Constant emphasis was made on the need to walk inside the school; I had mentioned this times without number in class and in school assemblies. What's the phrase? Practise what you preach. If only I had!

So, I was returning to class at 100mph down the corridor (the whole war effort was on hold so I had to hurry) and was homing in on the open classroom door when the adjacent classroom door opened and a small first-year pupil, a little girl, walked right in front of my door. Decision time: keep on going and she would be flattened; side step and I'd demolish the wall. In the end, realising I couldn't stop at the speed I was travelling, I chose a third option: I leapt over her before going through the door.

There were no problems with the leap – I was super-fit at that time – but a problem in my judgement of the door's height. The top of the doorframe was a wee bit lower than I'd anticipated. There was a dreadful thud, my head hit the doorframe and my legs shot forward, or so my students told me as I couldn't remember much following the impact. I hurtled through the air into the classroom about three-feet parallel to the floor, in a sort of reverse Superman flight. Finally I crashed into the side of my desk in front of the blackboard where I blacked out. How's that for an entrance?

The boys were used to some of my strange antics by now but this was something else. I'm told that I put my hand to the top of my head, which was bleeding heavily. Having regained consciousness, I tottered to my feet and staggered back down the corridor towards the school office.

My next recollection is of being comforted by another teacher. In my semi-conscious state, images of football and war flashed through my mind. I gleaned this information later, having subjected the attending staff to weird mutterings about planes dive-bombing the football pitch and tanks bearing down into the penalty area!

The cavalry arrived shortly after this in the guise of my sister, a nurse at the North Tees Hospital. She rushed from home, drove me to her workplace where, after several stitches in the gash in my head, I was kept in under observation overnight. The hospital staff asked what had happened and my flustered response was a bit vague, as you can imagine. Then, as the ward nurse folded up my jacket, 29p, a stick of chalk, my Acme 'thunderer' whistle and a few football card stickers I had taken off a pupil during a morning assembly fell out.

'Typical teacher,' I heard her mutter.

I didn't know what she was referring to and I didn't care. My head was pounding and I just wanted to sleep and forget what had happened.

My infamous leap became quite a talking point and was greatly exaggerated but there was no denying I had left my mark on the school. As far as I know, the dent in the wooden door frame is there to this day.

Following a day in hospital and a weekend's rest, I returned to school with one of the most embarrassing aspects of the whole affair awaiting me: writing up the accident-sheet report. It is always difficult to write up a purely factual report, devoid of emotion and feeling. I suppose it's rather like a police statement: 'I was proceeding along the corridor in a south-westerly direction when...'

*

Apart from trying to demolish the building, there were more positive aspects to school life. I am thinking now of three concerts I helped co-produce with Mrs Liz L., a most gifted teacher and friend. Although we produced quite a number of school musical events, some 'specials' come to mind: *Brer Rabbit; The Cowboy Concert,* and *Songs of the Sea*, were all memorable, well-received and set a high standard of singing, dancing, drama, costume and set design. All were performed within the constraints of a primary-school budget, but assisted by splendid support and encouragement from staff and parents. The *Brer Rabbit* concert was highly praised and we were invited to perform as part of a charity concert with senior schools and an adult choir in the Town Hall.

The Cowboy Concert was quite remarkable to me in that the response from the audience was tremendous; indeed, one of our VIP guests, well known in the town, commented that it was one of the best amateur shows he'd ever seen. He added, ' I'm not just talking about schools or children!' Praise indeed.

The *Songs of the Sea* concert was also of a high standard but tinged with sadness in a way, as I was shortly to be sailing away myself into uncharted waters as a head teacher. This was mentioned to the audience at the end of the final performance and, in the excitement and euphoria of a successful run, it was very difficult to hold back the tears.

I may not have been the most gifted teacher (but don't let me stop you debating the issue!) but I recall over the years some satisfying, productive and rewarding lessons in Maths, English, Science, History, etc., when everything seemed to be a success, pupils understood the points I had made and excellent work was produced. Of course, I admit that some seed did fall on stony ground!

There was the joy so many teachers experience of seeing children show improvement in their number work and reading ability after months of hard slog. Not once over the years, however, have ex-pupils come up to me and said, 'Sir, remember the scintillating work we did on addition of mixed fractions' or 'What about that story I wrote, when you raved about the fantastic punctuation!'

Not a chance! It just doesn't happen. Many ex-pupils have remarked on concerts we performed, football matches we played, occasions when things took place over and above the routine of school life. I am not demeaning the purpose of school but so many of the so-called frills and trimmings made the general school activities and life in school not just bearable but downright pleasurable.

Then came the day we amalgamated with the infants to become a 4–11 years primary school. The nature of the school changed as it always does; a new head teacher was appointed and periods of life during this transitional stage saw me in the role of acting head teacher. Thoughts of being a head were brought to the fore by many colleagues (just how desperately did they want rid of me?) and so the headship applications started to roll in. My thirst for power started to develop…

Little was I aware of what was in store!

5

Heady Days

'SHE'S GETTING TOO OLD AND
IS GOING TO PACK IT IN.'

Primary pupil

I believe the phrase is 'go for it'; well, that's what I was doing by filling in reams of dreadful forms that were part of the headship application process. Along with these time-consuming applications came the headship interviews, if your form was lucky enough to avoid the waste-paper basket. The basket was avoided at least six times before I landed a position.

Next was the pre-interview visit, always eye-opening, full of interest and speculation. Although I never declined an interview for a post following such visits, there were times at certain establishments when I strongly considered doing so and shuddered at the prospect of actually being appointed. They probably did likewise!

You are contacted by a brief note or quick phone call and you are invited to look around your prospective school, accompanied by the entourage of school advisor, school governor (usually the chairperson), perhaps a parent-governor, and the outgoing head teacher or the deputy head teacher. This is always a difficult assignment for deputies, especially if they are in the running.

The school tour is a delightful little ritual but beware – dangers are lurking behind every classroom door. This is the time when merit points can be gained and impressions can be made, hopefully favourable ones.

How do you set out your stall?

(a) Monopolise the most influential or vulnerable member of the party on the grand tour.

(b) Chatter with great enthusiasm to teachers and pupils within the school.

(c) Praise, with much pointing and similar body language, the display work on the walls, or

(d) The supreme sacrifice – show an interest in the boys' loos!

I've seen quite a lot of jockeying for pole position on these visits, if you'll excuse my mixed sporting metaphors.

Personally, I've found talking to the pupils most illuminating and informative. When asked about the school, they tend to shoot straight from the hip and tell it as it is, warts and all. On one of these tours, a pupil leaned over her table and, nodding towards the head teacher who was in the party, whispered in confidential tones and with great authority, 'Y'know why she's leaving? She's getting too old and is going to pack it in. She told me.'

On another occasion, a Year 6 boy said to me, 'I hope you come here. There's only women and they hate footy.'

What can you say? Perhaps the most revealing comment was when I praised a table of children for their poems displayed on the wall. 'Oh, we didn't do them, last year's class did.' Children move classes in July and it was mid-November at the time!

The visit is a prerequisite to the interview and, on occasion, the interview followed immediately. There was one visit when I'm so glad this was not the case.

During this particular visit we detoured to the detached jewel-in-the-crown swimming pool, sited in a long prefabricated building adjacent to the school play-yard. Naturally I was excited: a primary school with its own pool! I could picture splashing about with my own family after school when the pupils had all gone home. What a splendid facility for the whole school!

Sadly, my excitement and thoughts of what might be rather distracted me and I forgot the head teacher's instruction to look out for the footbath between the changing rooms and poolside. Splash! My highly polished black shoe got quite wet as the water rose above my left ankle. No one noticed, or at least they appeared not to, as I continued walking around with a soaking left foot. Thankfully I was wearing a dark suit but the tell-tale footprints and drips were rather visible as I manoeuvred myself to the back of the touring party. I did not get appointed. Perhaps, as I had already discovered to my cost, leaving one's mark isn't always advisable!

Preliminaries out of the way, it's time for the main event – the interview itself. The sacrificial lambs gather in a small anteroom. No matter where the ordeal takes place, in the school, the local education office, in a church vestry, it is still extremely stressful. I've sampled all three venues so I should know.

The nervous candidates draw lots for the batting order and the twitching and fiddling begins, the excitable chattering and slightly hysterical laughter. If you are last to be called, you sit as the earlier interviewees return and long to ask the exact nature of the questions. Thoughts play tricks in your mind: 'He looks fine now, obviously he did well...'; 'Look at her confident air – the job's cut and dried...'; 'Ah well, maybe next time...' Then your name is called out and you are led towards the interview room in a blind panic. You've forgotten everything you wanted to say, your mind is in a whirl. Straighten your tie, you're in!

You sit there while the panel members are introduced, up to a dozen people, all 'experts' whose sole intention to make you look foolish. They are seated in a horseshoe formation in front of your chair; the only thing missing seem to be the bright lights and thumbscrews! An author-itative voice states the well-chosen phrase, 'Just relax, we want you to give of your best.' No problem: ten of you get lost, the other two offer me the job and lead me to the nearest lounge bar! If only!

The questions come thick and fast and the answers are given thin and slowly. Minutes tick by as you blurt out your pseudo-spontaneous answers, answers you have been practising for days in the hope that they will fit some of the questions – although they still seem to come out all wrong.

Suddenly it's over and you are back in the waiting room. On with the fixed pose and pre-planned com-ments: 'Hmm, not too bad, not too bad at all. Was I in there a long time?' You lie through your teeth – you know to the very second. 'Forty minutes? Wow! It didn't seem that long,' or 'Only twenty minutes – they weren't very searching questions.' And you wait.

The wannabe heads have all been done and they wait.

The garrulous type who's been to more than a hundred interviews. He's seen it all before and has a gold medal and bar for long service in the face of danger... he waits.

The quiet, taciturn, young whizz kid – I ask you, what experience does he have – he waits.

The slim attractive lady, far too cultured for this Bash Street, corner-end school near the chip shop. She looks like an executive from Marks and Spencer's – I'd like to see her dealing with the 'sick bucket'… she waits.

The guy in the corner, full of wry comments, three-piece suit, bank manager/businessman type; *The Times* crossword almost completed. You aren't fooling anyone, mate. I looked at it when you were in your interview and the answers are blank or illegible… he waits

We all wait like characters from the board game *Cluedo*. Who will it be? Who's done it? Who's got it? Some game, some 'bored' game (yawn, yawn)!

What a long time, fifteen minutes, sixteen, seventeen, eighteen, nineteen, twenty… How long do they need?

The invitation for more coffee is refused. Someone speaks. 'Well, I'm off in ten minutes if they don't make up their minds.' (Liar! You'd wait two hours if you thought they'd give you the job.)

The door opens, a few polite words… come on, just say the name. The name is spoken and the named person looks surprised ('Who me?'… come on, you knew all along!) and wanders off to their destiny. Lesser mortals in the room, ego-rating zero, wait just a few more minutes before a face appears.

'Ladies and gentlemen, we have just offered the post of head teacher to Mr/Mrs/Ms Successful who has accepted the position. Thank you for your… etc., etc.' (You've failed, you're rubbish, go home, go back to your schools and don't bother any more!) The unsuccessful candidates depart swiftly.

'They wanted a woman, it was obvious.'

'He was a cert for the job from the word go.'

'It really wasn't for me.'

'I'm not bothering any more.'

'Of course, I'm happy where I am!'

But one day it happened and it was my name, and it was my day, and it was my position, and I was appointed head teacher. Just how do you equate that feeling? The sudden adrenaline rush akin to passing a driving test, holding up the FA Cup, scoring a winning run for England at Lords, winning an Olympic gold medal?

Whoa! Just a minute, old son, don't get carried away. You've been appointed as a head teacher of a school in Hartlepool. You won't be appearing on national TV, you won't be front-page news and questions will definitely not be asked in the House of Commons.

Yeah, but I feel great; that'll do for now.

So I enjoyed the congratulations, the cards, the kind words and, as I did so, I realised that this would be my last class of children as a class teacher. A very special bond, a special relationship that a class teacher has (or most certainly should have) for his own little group was disappearing. The rapport I'd had with classes for more than twenty years was ending soon, in fact in less than half a term, a few short weeks. I was moving on, swapping my classroom for a study, my auxiliary help for a secretary, my whistle for a telephone. It was a massive shift in responsibility and a time to focus on new horizons.

*

Where to begin in my new school? Well, taking heed of advice ('hurry slowly' was one pearl of wisdom), I settled in slowly, doing little talking but much listening and observing. There was so much to hear and so much more to see, and both activities were beneficial. I was fortunate that the school was running smoothly; it had had a competent and experienced head, who was moving on to a headship in a bigger school down the road. The deputy head I inherited was young, keen and full of fresh ideas; the secretary and caretaker had been around for years. With these folk around me, I was pleased to be phased in rather gently. I had even made my first appointment before I left my previous school. She was a wonderful young lady who proved to be one of the best appointments of quite a number I was privileged to make over the years.

It was a compact school with experienced staff, though not too long in the tooth, and things ran smoothly. I tried to introduce new initiatives gradually and without stress and I got used to the routines and practices of the school before changes were made. One of the things I really enjoyed was taking the morning assemblies and communicating with the whole school to develop a feeling of togetherness.

One assembly I planned during the first autumn term was to prove interesting in how it was structured!

Thumbing through a book called *Day by Day*, I came upon a story called 'Honesty' and decided I would read this to the assembled school. It would feature an 'honest' pupil that I would select using my own little scheme.

I decided to place a one-pound coin on the hall floor on the Monday morning, en route from the classes to the secretary's office, which was situated next to mine. The idea was that pupils crossing the hall on the first day of the week with registers, dinner-money tins, school bank books or parental permission slips for a trip to Outer Mongolia would notice the coin and one of them would show honesty by handing it in.

With my cunning plan prepared, I placed the coin on the floor just after ten past nine, when all the pupils were in their rooms and then I waited. Children were soon leaving their classrooms to take registers, forms and money tins to the office, while I waited for the honest pupil. 'Ah well, it wasn't a bad idea,' I thought, as the clock ticked on; perhaps the coin had been kicked accidentally underneath the stacked chairs in the corner of the hall. Then, at almost 9.30, a few minutes before I was due to take the assembly, minus my honest guinea pig, there was a knock on my door.

A small Year 4 boy (about eight years old) came in clutching the coin.

'I found this in the hall, Mr Cross. Mrs Dixon said I had to bring it to you.'

What a delight! I came from behind my desk, gave him a hug and lifted him towards the ceiling. 'Well done, young man,' I said joyfully. 'You are to be the star of this morning's assembly.'

He was indeed; however, there was a twist in the tale. He had in fact been late, not for the first time since the beginning of the school year, and had been sent to me for a telling-off for being a persistent latecomer! Some reward for being late, I thought, but I had made a promise and, in spite of his class teacher's puzzled looks, he was the main feature of the morning assembly. The telling-off – well, that came later in the day!

A spin-off to the story was that in the days that followed there was an increased number of pupils wanting to take messages, registers and so forth to the office at the beginning of the school day. Teachers commented on how their children sat up smartly and got on with their work so as to be chosen to do these early morning duties. It was certainly interesting for some days after the 'honest' assembly to watch pupils scanning the floor for more coins. Alas for those on the lookout, I did not do it again; I quit whilst I was ahead.

Weeks and months went by with assemblies, planning meetings, letters to parents, working, getting to know pupils and staff and I was getting accustomed to being head of the school. It was not all plain sailing, I assure you!

My philosophy, as the sign in my room stated, was: 'Not above you or below you, but with you'. This was a team thing; it was not *my* school but *our* school and I tried to give respect and recognition to everyone, from the youngest pupil to the most senior and experienced member of staff, from the most demanding parent to the chair of governors (they could be demanding too!). Any success the school enjoyed was due to the efforts and endeavours of the whole school community.

I rarely entered the building after 7.30am and rarely left before 6pm during those early headship years. There was such a lot to take on board. My relaxation was running the school football team; it brought an extra workload but I found it an effective way of winding down. What a surprise! The main time for practice matches and competitive games was on a Friday after school, when most staff were leaving school earlier than usual and getting ready for a well-earned weekend break.

Donning a tracksuit and getting outside on the field or into the sports hall was good therapy, as my fitness levels were declining rapidly. However, running a school imposed severe time limitations and my football coaching often had to be fitted in where possible. In spite of this, I was still able to develop some useful footballers with quite a degree of success.

There was a high price to be paid for this sporting involvement. I would stagger out of school at a late hour with a stack of administration work I could have attended to in my office instead of getting hot, sweaty and muddy – and, of course, I would have avoided the infamous touchline drama!

*

It was about 5.15pm midweek and I was holding a rare non-Friday football practice because of a forthcoming county cup quarter-final. As the practice was in full flow, I was summoned to the touchline by a tall, strongly built man who was clearly rather angry and agitated. He demanded that I leave the game and speak to him in school. When I explained that I couldn't leave the pupils without supervision, he became more annoyed.

Suddenly I realised what was happening and why he was here; about half an hour earlier I had exchanged words with a teenage boy with a large dog who had been interfering with our practice. This was not an uncommon occurrence; at various times during the term we'd had groups of youths, unaccompanied dogs, golfers and straying motor bikers on our hallowed turf. This was the boy's dad!

To cut a long and painful story short, he confronted me at the side of the pitch and I found myself on the ground due to the fact that his forehead was harder than mine! As I rose to my feet to try and speak to him again, he strode away and I was left feeling quite shaken. In my groggy state I was assisted off the field by a helpful grandparent who, along with the school caretaker and a member of the teaching staff, attended to the players' and my needs.

Against my wishes, the police were informed and sent for, which made me delay driving home as I needed recovery time. Ironically, although I was not aware of it at the time, the man who had confronted me happened to be the father of not only the youth on the touchline but one of the players in the practice game! I had, in fact, been trying to stop his eldest boy from spoiling his youngest boy's football practice. It was a lose-lose situation.

The matter was later resolved and the man in question, along with his wife, met with me in my office. He shook hands with me after having apologised. He had a third son who also played in the school team that reached a county-cup final; Dad was there, supporting from the touchline and he and I eventually had a much-improved relationship.

In spite of the police getting involved, resulting in a photo-file of the bruised forehead, I was foolish enough to return to school the following day. I was not badly injured, more shocked than anything else, though a day off school would have been a wise move. I wanted to be the tough guy, the macho man, I suppose.

Two things happened, one that was slightly humorous and one that was distinctly not:

(1) On the morning of my return, I was passing through the cloakroom as children were coming in to school and overheard the tail end of a remark: '…Got beaten up last night.' 'Bang goes my street-cred,' I thought.

(2) Midway through the morning there was a heavy banging on my door. Who on earth was that? I was not in the best of spirits and snatched open the door, expecting to scold a pupil for knocking furiously and not having seen the school secretary before disturbing me. Would you believe it: there, towering in the doorframe, was a

giant of a man. 'Oh no!' I thought. 'Someone else has it in for me!' I was tempted to slam the door shut and take refuge behind my desk. Thankfully I resisted this course of action and, gazing into his chest, I heard him say in a slow, ponderous way, 'Could I have the keys for the gate to the field?' It was one of the education authority gardeners; he was a massive Swedish chap, here to cut the grass with his gang-mower. Little did he realise how close he was to bringing on a severe heart attack!

*

Happily, many on-field memories were good. During the first two years, our soccer team won the 'A' Division Championship Shield both seasons, which was quite a feat for any school. To celebrate this achievement one of our parents, who had a friend of a friend in the wedding-hire car business, arranged for a white Rolls Royce to take the champions around the estate. So, on the morning of the appointed day, the football squad were driven in two groups in splendour around the local area, holding the trophy and waving to the thousands of supporters lining the roads. Well, not really; the local man walking his dog and the pensioners queuing outside the post office were rather curious, and some of the pedestrians did wave!

As I mentioned earlier, I had an excellent hardworking staff and the school was running well. On occasion, I had to leave the premises during the day and visit the town centre, sometimes to go to the bank or shopping arcade for various school sundries. These visits were a welcome break from the pressures of school life and I was often on my own; having too many staff away from school during the course of a busy working day was not practical and not recommended.

One lunchtime I needed to leave school together with my deputy to provide specimen signatures for banking purposes. Rarely did the head and deputy leave school during working hours (lunchtime for senior staff are often working hours), so we rushed along to the town centre, joking about how there would be a mini-disaster during our absence. Banking transactions completed, we drove back to school with only five minutes to spare before the 1pm start bell. Steve needed to be back to teach his class; I had to prepare for a meeting at 1.45pm. There was no time to spare but no real problems.

The road we were travelling back to school was a busy two-way thoroughfare. It shouldn't have taken long but suddenly the vehicles started to back up and we slowed and we stopped.

The two or three minutes seemed like hours as we fidgeted and waited impatiently. Finally we decided that action was needed and I performed a splendid U-turn to get us away from the snarl up. Almost a hundred metres down the road I took a side turn-off, hoping to thread my way past the traffic hazard. Alas, I was not alone! Other cars were trying the same ploy, seeking to avoid what I later discovered was a major emergency road blockage.

We huffed and puffed as we were held up in several places in an unknown housing estate, getting ourselves into a maze of streets, cul-de-sacs and no-entry roads. The final straw was turning into another side road and finding ourselves behind a funeral procession that was just start-ing off. Two black limousines were slowly gliding behind the hearse and, right at the front, a tall man with black frock coat and top hat was walking at a snail's pace.

By now it was almost 1.30pm. Would we get back to school before home time? I was sure there would be chaos in the dining hall, major warfare, one of the dinner supervisors 'eaten up', a serious accident and other staff late because of the traffic hold up. Remember, there were no mobile phones to contact school in those days.

How long was this man going to keep walking, ever so slowly, in front of the cars?

We sat there, hot, bothered and totally frustrated. Finally we resigned ourselves to having been put on the missing-persons' list and saw the funny side of it. We started laughing hysterically. As other cars built up behind us, we found the situation even funnier, and thoughts of cars in front of us with mourners in tears and now us in tears just made things worse. Disrespectful though it seems, we were both helpless with laughter. Eventually we gave the funeral cortege the slip and reached home base over an hour late, sides aching with laughter and totally drained from the experience. At least everything was in one piece at school; staff had adapted to the AWOL personnel. But there were strange portents on the horizon and a big shock was to arrive out of the blue that changed things for all of us!

I was attending a head-teachers' meeting when a rather young and inexperienced education officer joined a small group of us chatting over coffee and a biscuit during a welcome break in the proceedings. The usual conversations were flowing: external vandalism in our schools; budgetary problems; staffing issues, etc., when the young man turned to me and said in a casual throw-away style, 'You'll be all getting set for your new school, then?'

I don't know why but a sort of sixth sense made me take his arm and usher him away from the group towards a quiet area. It was the way he said it and the way my colleagues seemed interested; I realised that something was about to happen that I was not aware of.

'I think we'd better have a chat' I said hurriedly.

He chatted alright, although he had little specific information. Perhaps he realised he had already said enough! The main thrust was that our junior school and the adjacent infant and nursery school were to be amalgamated to create a new primary school with more than 500 pupils, the last one to be developed in the authority.

Yes, things were in for a change… how big and traumatic I was soon to discover.

6

Can You See the Join?

'GIRLS WEAR PINK UNDERPANTS'

A nursery pupil

Sunday evenings for the majority of Monday-to-Friday employees, certainly teachers, are times for preparing mentally for the week ahead, for girding one's loins, a time when most people will, however briefly, ponder the forthcoming week's activities.

The particular Sunday I have in mind had nothing to do with musing, just mopping... I was in an ex-infant teachers' staffroom, peeling wallpaper, with a water pipe sticking out of the wall in the corner and three remaining tiles that had been the splash-back for the sink. This was to be my room, the headmaster's study, the nerve-centre of the school, where key decisions would be made affecting the lives of 500 children and their families – and it was a mess! And we opened as a new school in two days' time!

What an inheritance! Not totally unexpected, of course, as in July when the school year ended and we ceased to function as separate infant and junior schools, plans had been made with wild, unrealistic optimism. It was supposed to be very simple. Everything – and I mean everything – from the junior school was crated into huge blue-plastic storage boxes and transferred, together with desks, tables, cupboards, pianos, etc., into the infant-school hall. This job was to be completed by the removal men at the start of the long summer holiday, before a total rewiring of the junior school. During the rest of the holiday, a few holes would be knocked in walls, one classroom was to be converted into a staffroom and a pupil toilet block was to be transformed into a female staff toilet block. Now what could be simpler? I am not a builder but I had grave doubts, even though I was promised – oh how I was promised!

Four weeks into the six-week holiday break, I visited the school, which had changed from a separate infant and junior school bombsite to a primary-school bombsite!

In the two days prior to breaking up for the summer, crates and furniture were stacked and labelled ready for the move. We had little time for reminiscing. The sight that hit me was incredible. In the infant hall, almost from floor to ceiling and wall to wall, there was an accumulation of equipment and furniture. On the junior school side it was even worse: wires dangling from classroom ceilings; a workshop situation in the main hall with two workbenches, tools and coils of electrical cable. Even the workmen's obligatory radio gave me cause for alarm; it was blasting out pop music, a Bonnie Tyler number 'It's a Heartache'. How prophetic was that? Help! What is happening here? This will never be ready in time!

So, let's forward again to the Sunday evening and the floor mopping. I was determined that at least there would be one area of the school that was dust free. Not that I was fussy or of the opinion that I came first before the children and staff, but there would be many visitors to our new school and a reasonable area for greeting them would be nice – before they changed into hard-hats, boiler suits, face masks and goggles!

Staff would be arriving back tomorrow, many having visited school the previous week after having left in a shell-shocked dusty state and making comments that I wouldn't dare to repeat. Living out of the town, I received numerous phone calls that particular week which confirmed their alarm and mine.

'Have you been in?'

'You should see it!'

I had been in… I had seen it!

Our initial staff meeting was not in our new staffroom but in one of the classrooms on the infant side. As I was delivering my keynote address, my words of wisdom, two huge Pickfords' removal vans bounced over the school field, transferring back the paraphernalia to the junior side. I felt like the opposition manager of a team playing against Manchester United away from home in the FA Cup losing 4–0 at half-time and trying to inspire second-half success.

The staff were magnificent and worked long and hard trying to sort out their teaching areas as hundreds of blue crates of equipment were dumped in classrooms. Furniture that had been colour coded was scattered around.

'I'm looking for a purple table.'

'Anyone seen a blue desk?'

'I don't know. I've lost my yellow crate with all my maths equipment!'

If it hadn't been so serious it would have made us laugh as though we were watching a *Carry On* film… *Carry On Amalgamating*!

Could anything get worse? Well, as the two large vans backed up to the double-entrance doors off the junior yard, their weight cracked several paving stones near the doors. The newly installed ladies toilets suddenly refused to flush and the radiator in my room started leaking. Oh yes, things could get worse!

This was crisis management. This was the *Titanic* in dire peril on its maiden voyage. This was Britain at the onset of World War II, the darkest hour. And this particular Winston Churchill had delivered his stirring speech to the troops. Loins were girded; now it was crunch time. The shrill whistle blew; 'Over the top lads, up and at 'em!' Would our staff be ready for the battle?

We needed a week to sort it all out. We gained two days and, instead of the pupils returning on the Tuesday, they returned on the Thursday thanks to a monumental effort from both teaching and non-teaching staff.

It's amazing how perspectives change! We had a group of education officials tour the school, 'reviewing the situation' (to quote Fagin) on the Tuesday evening. The rooms were full of storage crates, unpacked and seriously wobbling, three or four boxes high at the side of each classroom. It was suggested that pupils could access these resources during the working day. No chance, not our pupils! We had our challenging types but even they didn't deserve to have a crate bounced off their heads!

One of the visiting education group had signed a health and safety circular some months earlier, which requested schools withdraw glass test tubes from their science stock because of the danger. Schools had to comply rigorously! As I say, how perspectives change when it suits!

Another hard slog of a day and, in spite of most class-rooms still having a motley assortment of crates and un-sorted boxes, we opened our doors to the pupils two days later than expected. I'm sure our pupils were heartbroken! At least we had gained publicity of a sort, with the head-lines in the local paper reading: *School Locks Out Pupils*, referring to the extra days we needed. The accompanying photo next to the article showed a lone parent flanked on either side by two glum-faced pupils. One of our parents suggested that the photographer should have toured the estate to snap scores of less glum pupils, ecstatic at having gained two extra days' holiday. Thankfully, such was our good relationship with the parents that 99% were grateful for our efforts and the headlines were amended a few days later to praise the sterling work of staff. Things would get better and over the weeks, months and years that followed they did.

*

Our challenges were remarkable. Staff from two very different schools were trying to gel as one, not an easy task at the best of times, plus they faced a new system of delegated budget arrangements, new National Curriculum initiatives and the introduction of an appraisal system.

Anyone for tennis?

No staff could have worked harder in that first year and so many objectives were achieved. Apart from coming to terms with fusing together separate school educational schemes and working practices, we moved into our new staffroom. Toilets were fixed, rooms created, fences erected, security systems installed and we suddenly found we had made it to July, the end of the first school year! At last the long summer holidays arrived and surprise, surprise, this summer holiday the infant side of the school was to be totally rewired. NO! Not the blue boxes, the vans, the dust, the coloured labels again.

Oh yes indeed! I didn't believe it! But I had to. It was true!

*

Vandalism and break-ins were a constant problem and, although security alarms and high metal-grille fencing were in place, over the course of the early years it was still an on-going challenge. On one sad occasion a two-classroom block, separate from the main school by a few yards, was set on fire and totally destroyed. Some mindless hooligans attacked firemen and police personnel attending the fire, with one unfortunate PC being subjected to physical abuse and receiving cuts and bruises to his face.

The photos of the inferno were quite dramatic, capturing the blaze at its height; however, when I arrived much of the smoke and flames had died down leaving the blackened shell of the building. I had been relaxing in my bath at home when I received the news but arrived at the scene within half an hour. The school yard was crowded with spectators. Various fire officers, education officials and a county architect met with me and a few senior staff in an adjoining main-site classroom. Had the firemen been delayed by a few minutes, I was told, the main school block would have been severely damaged. As it was, the room we were in had been partially burned, with several windows cracked and shattered with the heat, alongside fascia boards charred black.

Discussion was under way regarding temporary measures, safety aspects and contingency plans when a parental head stuck itself very dangerously through one of the broken and jagged window panes.

'Well, is the school still open tomorrow then?'

'Yes,' I sighed. 'We shall be open tomorrow!'

We were!

*

On the whole, our parents were wonderfully supportive of the school and their children; most parents are provided that they are informed, encouraged and made welcome. Sadly, they did not always warm to each other. I can recall more than one occasion when there were squabbles in the school yard, one of which led to fisticuffs and grappling on the floor! I have always encouraged parental activity within school and have involved myself most times but on this particular day I withdrew; there were some challenges I could do without!

Sometimes there are occasions when parents challenge you full on and there's just no escape. Such was the case when an argument arose between two mums, one rather small and the other huge! Their disagreement started in one of the classrooms separate from the main building and developed with such ferocity that threats were made loud and angrily. The verbals ended in Mrs Small being chased across the yard by Mrs Huge into the main school; thanks to our internal phone system, I was warned of the tornado approaching and that the office area, my room in particular, might be a likely sanctuary for 'Mrs Small'.

No sooner had I put the phone down than the chased parent burst open my door and ran behind my chair to huddle down behind my waste-paper bin in the corner. Seconds later the room darkened as the second parent slammed back the door and towered towards me, as I was the obstacle betwixt both parents.

My desk being end on to a wall, I was blocking the route of the aggressive Mrs Huge. Raising my arms, I bellowed, 'Get out!'

Now, this was not my normal first line of approach to parents, you understand, but on this occasion it seemed highly appropriate to halt the raging rhino. It did stop her in her tracks and within moments the entourage of staff, chasing her like silent-movie cops, were able to shepherd the large lady away to the calm of the deputy head's room. There she was soothed and settled down via the magic of tea, biscuits and my right-hand person, who was an expert at dealing with such calamities.

Thankfully my screaming had had the desired shock effect otherwise, as she was double my weight, I could have been powered through the large window behind my desk. In scenarios such as these I would ask myself, 'What kind of staff do I need? Subject specialists or nightclub bouncers?'

*

My contact with parents, mums in particular, was increasing due to my primary-head teacher status and the nursery within our school. I've always thought it rather sad that parental involvement declines so rapidly as pupils move up the school. Perhaps the presence – or at least the threat of the presence – of parents in the comprehensive school would help with some discipline problems.

Our school had the nursery as a central link between the two main halls and teaching blocks. Such was the geography of the building that I had to pass through the nursery regularly during the day. Nursery children being as they are, I was rarely ignored on my travels through their area and far too often I was late for meetings due to being caught up in their activities. I was unable to resist them showing me their latest artistic creation or sharing a 'cup of tea' and a 'sandwich' in the 'home corner' (pretend ones, of course!).

There was the day I was sidetracked yet again on my travels through the nursery, this time in the library area.

Three boys happened to be looking at a picture book. A disagreement arose as to whether the picture of the person riding a bike showed a boy or a girl. The rider was wearing jeans and had close-cropped hair. I knew I shouldn't have got involved, especially as the boy/girl differences started.

'What's the difference between a boy and a girl?' I was asked in a roundabout sort of way. I was deciding how to frame my response when the little chap holding the picture book saved me a job as he uttered a super definitive statement that I thought I would use in the future. In a loud voice, with all the sureness of a four year old, he said, 'I know, girls wear pink underpants!'

His little friends accepted that and they carried on sharing the picture book together. I escaped with a giggle. How simple, why didn't I think of that? My answer could not have been accepted more readily, I'm sure.

Not all the memorable experiences were bound up with pupils or parents, and some of the visitors to school brought their own special magic.

The friend of one of the cleaning ladies who brought in his thirty-foot python to school to show the children; now why was I absent that day, I wonder?

The bank manager who, smartly dressed and super confident in my office, found it almost impossible to keep control and attention in the school hall in front of the assembled school. Indeed, he seemed close to collapsing!

Then there was Brian Blessed. Yes, Brian Blessed, international celebrity of stage and screen. Think of the deep sonorous voice, think of *Z Cars* if you're old enough! Yes, that Brian Blessed, in our school. What a coup!

The story of his visit stemmed from months of effort in creating a library within the school, not a little area in the corner of a room with a few bookcases and posters on the wall. No, we wanted a proper library, a room given over to books, tables and comfortable chairs, with the express purpose of making a statement that books were important in our school, in our studies, in our lives.

We were all working hard to develop a new reading scheme through the school; our focus was on literacy, so we wanted to create a super library. Alarming statistics are thrown up annually about adult non-readers, school leavers unable to read accurately, children showing little or no interest in reading books. Well, we may be providing numbers within those figures but at least we were going to try and alter things.

Although it meant change and disruption yet again, the idea developed splendidly with parents, governors, friends of the school – yes, we did have some!– all donating money and books, giving their time running discos, fashion shows and bingo nights. My bingo calling was a joy to behold: 'Two thin ladies, number 11; a tin of Heinz, number 57.' Local firms donated carpets and curtains and bookcases were bought or made; our caretaker, Rob, saved us hundreds of pounds with his efforts. Books were assembled and things were coming together.

We needed an official opening, someone to open our new library – perhaps a famous, favourite author.

We needed to be careful, having once experienced a most painful afternoon when an author came to talk about the children's books he had written. If only he had left us the books to read. Poor man, he could write books well enough but when it came to talking to children, telling them about his work, he bored the pants off them. So we decided to leave the author idea!

Maybe someone in the public eye; a celebrity who had recently written a book? On reflection perhaps not, as some of the revelations in certain books, especially of the sporting type, would bring controversy. We'd had enough stones thrown through our windows by local vandals; we certainly didn't want to attract a national salvo of missiles by inviting someone who might say something undesirable.

Then one evening, sitting at home reading a newspaper, I noticed a publicity piece in the entertainments column about a show coming to Darlington Civic Theatre, *The Wizard of Oz*. Great film, great book; I'd read it to my own boys when they were small. We all had our favourite characters. I just loved the Scarecrow in the film and the song 'If I Only Had a Heart'. Reading further, I noticed the name of one of the stars of this show was Brian Blessed. He was just the person to open our library! I had a hunch he would do it.

I don't always have the greatest of ideas (you will have come to this conclusion quite readily in Chapter 1 of this book!) but I had a gut feeling that this guy, from what I had seen and heard, was a genuine person, ideal for the task. Boy, I could not have made a better choice.

Although initially I kept my thoughts very much to myself, my biggest fear was that a man of his stature might be far too busy to bother with our little school and its puny efforts. I was so wrong and my judgement on this score was wide of the mark; I totally underestimated what sort of person we were dealing with. So, the letters were written, a few phone calls made, and with many 'have I done the right thing?' thoughts, we awaited the big fella coming to open our library.

If you get the impression that Brian Blessed is loud, larger than life and imposing, you're dead right. In addition, throw in generous and pretty damn special! In spite of him being busy and in demand, he gave up a full morning to give us all a wonderful time.

From the moment he stepped into the school, he was so full of charisma and charm yet the sort of person you could get on with quite easily. He had the air of being a star without giving you the impression of being different. It's difficult to explain but spend five minutes in his company and you will know what I mean!

It was a privilege to share the assembly time with him prior to him opening the library. He talked to the children and staff so naturally and brought a warmth and joy to the day. Especially important was his contribution to staff morale which, over the past years, had hardly been sky high. We have our 'failing teachers' and 'failing schools', that's fair enough and I'll accept that label stuck on many of our colleagues and schools; but let's start naming other institutions: 'failing solicitors', 'failing bank managers', 'failing plumbers', etc.

Even if teachers are lowered to the basic level of 'child minders', you ask parents towards the end of the six-week holiday period about the value of schools and teachers. 'I'll be glad when you're back at school!' rings out the stressed-out parent's voice.

'But with a "failing teacher" and in a "failing school",' pipes up the child.

'I don't care if you're writing with your finger in the chalk dust, I'll be glad when you're out from under my feet and back at school!'

Sorry about that… er, as I was saying…

Brian Blessed, following a clowning-about session with me and a humorous poem we shared, went on to speak to us about how much he valued his school and teachers. He did us all a power of good; those who were there in the hall that magical morning would remember the experience for a long, long time.

Let's face it, he was visiting a rather insignificant little school (I speak here of the possible perspective of other people, not ours!) in a less than high-profile north-eastern town and yet he gave one hundred per cent of himself with such enthusiasm and energy. A big man, a big day in our school.

*

A few days after BB's visit, we were still on a high when a most distressing incident happened on our school field. I was out taking a football games lesson with our older pupils (as you will have gathered I wasn't always stuck behind my desk) when a group of youths rounded the corner of the comprehensive school, bordering our field. They had with them a bull terrier that was off its lead.

Children chasing a football, a dog unleashed – a recipe for problems. Shades of the film *Jaws*; you remember the scene, children splashing about in the water, the shark suddenly attracted…

My reckoning was correct and, after a few freeze-frame seconds, the animal darted towards us. Most of the children, mainly boys, were unaware of the dog racing towards them and were concentrating on playing the game – I had taught them well. As the terrier started barking, their attention suddenly strayed.

Should we run away? Try to ignore the dog? It was a tough call to make. Eventually I decided. 'Stand still!' I yelled at the top of my voice, drowning out the shouts of the lads trying to call back their dog.

The players – and I – all stood still as the terrier wove between our multi-coloured legs, snapping and snarling. Suddenly the object of our desire a few seconds ago – the football – had rolled to a halt and sat there rather sad and unwanted.

'Go for the ball, you stupid dog! There's an open goal ahead, no one will challenge you.' As we stood there for what seemed a very long time I shouted once more, this time at the youths, 'Come on, get rid of this thing!'

One of the group raced over towards us as we stood there like a team of table-soccer figures. Too late, however, as the creature brushed against my leg and zoomed in on a poor unfortunate pupil, sinking its teeth into his calf muscle. Then I moved, joined within seconds by the racing youth and his mates. Sadly the dog would not let go and was lifted up bodily, still attached to the football-er's leg. The screams of the boy were agonising as the dog was pummelled by the youths in an effort to force it to release its grip. Eventually the animal slackened its jaws and was pulled away, though the black nylon threads of the player's sock were still attached to its jaws as the dog was dragged off. They were tangled around its teeth and still pulling a few feet away from the boy's sock, finally snapping with a ping as the dog was freed.

Still in a state of shock, we all started responding. The kids were great. I sent one to the school office to get the staff to phone for an ambulance; the rest just sat on the grass without fuss as I tended Paul, the injured footballer. What a brave lad. He was still in shock as I carried him into school, shouting towards the group with the dog, 'You – school – tomorrow!' I think they knew what I meant! Indeed the dog owner did turn up the following day.

Paul was taken to the hospital but was back at school the next day, proudly displaying his badge of honour: two pairs of bright-red puncture marks on the back of his leg. He hadn't even needed stitches!

As to why the dog attacked Paul in particular, when there were so many other juicy legs available, we shall never know; suffice to say he was the only one wearing a Manchester United strip! We just had to assume the dog was of the Manchester terrier breed and one obviously favouring City rather than the 'Reds'. It certainly wasn't funny at the time and we were quite shocked but tried to see the humour of what happened, especially as a week or two's hindsight meant we could venture on to the games field without too much stress. Jokingly we suggested Paul should wear two pairs of shin pads, one protecting his shins and the other the back of his legs!

*

Meanwhile, back in the library resources were being added daily and classes were timetabled to use this super facility – and, of course, it was an ideal place for our governors' meeting. Enter Mr G.!

Now I had a good relationship with our governors; it was not difficult really as, over the years, we had been blessed with a wonderful body of people who worked so well with us. There were always, of course, the few whom we met after their appointment but were never seen again after the initial meeting! Not only was the main body of governors a good bunch but crucially, over the years, the chair of governors' position was filled with some very supportive and school/teacher friendly people. In any situation, it was comforting to know that they were on the end of the phone for help, guidance and support. As things happened so frequently, there were many situations!

So to Mr G. He was a governor, an elderly, kindly, friendly chap and lovely to talk with regarding any aspect of school life, an ideal sounding board. Into my office he staggered one morning with a huge cardboard box carefully packed with a superb assortment of handcrafted Ancient Egyptian figurines. It must have taken hundreds of hours to shape and paint these delicate figures of upright poses, kneeling figures, camels with riders (and some without), ladies carrying water pots on their heads and shoulders and dark-skinned Arabs with menacing eyes brandishing curved daggers. It was a collection of figures that would have graced the local museum and Mr G. wanted us to have them for display in our library as a permanent feature. What a wonderful gesture – but surely these artefacts were too special for our library? No, he would have none of it; he wanted our school to have them.

As each figure was lovingly unwrapped and placed on the coffee table in my room, I enthused about how wonderful they were, perhaps a wee bit OTT, but they were exceptional. 'These are truly magnificent, Mr G. I just can't thank you enough. We'll treasure these figures, put them in a glass-fronted cabinet. Most certainly we shall have them on display for the next governors' meeting.'

Oh, I was so gushing in my praise, but why not? I was genuinely grateful and excited at such a splendid acquisition for the school; so excited, in fact, that after he had replaced the figures in the box and left my room, I couldn't wait to show the treasures to my deputy. Like an excited child with a present from Santa, I rushed out of my room along the corridor to my colleague's room – then disaster! I lost my footing, stumbled and the box flew into the air. I gasped out loud as the precious figures shot out of the box and into space, tumbling about before my eyes. As I fell on my knees, unable to retrieve the situation, the figurines seemed to fall in slow motion, spreading in a graceful semi-circular arc in front of my shocked gaze.

Shock horror! 'We'll really treasure them…'

'Put them in a glass-fronted case…'

'On display at the next governors' meeting…'

Why, oh why, was I so over-enthusiastic? As I knelt there on the floor, surrounded by the Egyptian carnage, camels minus humps, broken water pots, severed heads, arms and legs missing from torsos, I was in despair. Then it just seemed so funny; apologies for my apparent disrespect, but there is a fine line between success and failure and between laughter and tears. I burst into hysterical laughter, so loudly that my deputy came out of her office. She must have thought, 'Hello, he's finally flipped this time.'

When I was able, through my laughter, to explain what had happened she also saw the humour in the situation. As we gathered together the body parts, we were both helpless with giggles.

Safely back in my room, tears almost dry, we surveyed the bits and pieces. 'What are we going to do?' I groaned.

'Correction,' she replied. 'What are *you* going to do?'

How's that for teamwork? No, she did help as I knew she would, but not before another outburst of laughter as my secretary walked in on the scene and creased up after hearing the tale. Both with a wicked sense of humour, I think part of their laughter was because of the predicament I had got myself in to!

Eventually my sides stopped aching, my tears dried up and it was cold-light-of-day time. Thanks to my office colleagues, we carted the box to a member of staff who they thought was an expert at sticking things together. She was, and in a few days the dismembered bodies were joined up once more. Panic over... well almost. There was the small matter of the governors' meeting!

The figures went on display, smothered with posters, books and labels, so many labels that we got away with it! One or two of the figures were in such a bad state that they were impossible to repair and had to be binned. Much sadder, however, was that this lovely library, packed full of resources, was razed to the ground along with all of the buildings in the old junior school side of the site about a year after I retired. A very sad day indeed, a day when real tears were shed.

7

Can I Help You?

'CHILDREN DON'T CARE HOW MUCH YOU KNOW BUT THEY KNOW HOW MUCH YOU CARE!'

Behind every successful man there's a woman, or so the saying goes. Well in my case, I'm not so sure about the successful man bit, but I am about the woman – or women! Let me explain! There were two: one was my wife, long-suffering with a husband who worked far too long hours; then there was my working partner at school. She was also long-suffering and worked hours that were far too long. You can see the pattern developing here!

I was fortunate in having both these lovely ladies, so supportive, so encouraging and so very special. My working partner, the deputy head Mrs M., was magnificent and yet what a traumatic beginning we had. Incidentally Mr M., my working partner's husband, was a lovely man; he was also long-suffering as his wife worked far too lengthy hours… I told you there was a pattern!

Imagine, if you will, the situation as we changed from being two separate schools into a single primary school. Two head teachers and two deputy heads. The head of the infant school was of retirement age, a pity really as she was a lovely, jolly person, much loved by pupils and staff, a lady who had helped me settle in as a very green head when I was appointed next door to the juniors.

95

So that left me as head with two deputies. The problem resolved itself as my number two in the juniors went to higher things and was appointed a head teacher, leaving me with the infant deputy head, Mrs M.

I had no say in the matter but she had no choice either. We were stuck with each other, as it were!

As spokesperson for the infant staff now that the infant head had gone, she naturally fought her corner for her colleagues, whilst I had a loyalty to my former junior staff who were still with me. Naturally both sets of staff had different ways of operating and, although suspicions and concerns regularly arose as one would expect during the first few months, in time they disappeared. The teachers became colleagues and the colleagues became friends.

To be fair, Joyce and I had little time to exchange social chit-chat during those early days of amalgamation. It was 100mph stuff with tin hats worn and up to our knees in muck and bullets! Eventually there were incidents that brought us to our knees, often with effort and often with laughter; the tears and laughter as much as anything helped develop a special bond between us. The flames of adversity, quite literally on occasions (the arson attacks), made us warm to each other – no pun intended! Standing together in the glass amid the debris of vandalism, standing shoulder to shoulder against aggression and violence, fuses a common partnership... well, it did with us.

Joyce had some interesting tales to tell of days gone by and things that had happened to her... Ah, a kindred spirit.

I recall her telling of the morning when she was delivering Harvest Festival produce to the local residents, following the school assembly. Accompanied by a group of six to seven year olds, she met one old man who stooped at the door to gratefully accept the food parcel. 'Would you like to see my wife?' he asked.

Not wishing to be unfriendly, our Joyce stepped into the front room expecting to be greeted by the gentleman's white-haired, old wife. She was white-haired alright; she was also very white faced and very dead, laid out in her coffin in the room! The sight took my colleague by surprise but fortunately not the children; at the first glimpse, she turned on her heel, collected the trailing group of children and beat a hasty retreat! I'm sure she conducted herself with the greatest of dignity and would have said a polite goodbye! I thought these sort of things only happened to me – yes, she was a kindred spirit indeed.

This, along with so many experiences that came from working with young children, gave her the 'read the book, got the tee-shirt' status. The way she handled things that would have fazed a much younger, allegedly with-it teacher, was no surprise. Take the case of the three intruders…

We were assembled in the hall one morning with me doing my story at the front, the children hanging on my every word.

'You, boy, stop fiddling with your shoe lace…'

'Sarah leave Karen's hair alone…' Well, most of them were listening!

As the assembly continued, Joyce suddenly left her chair at the side of the hall and disappeared through one of the doors at the side of the front of the stage. Although no one else was aware of her reasons, she had gone out to challenge three youths who had walked into the school via the back doors. They appeared to be up to no good, possibly looking for a quick snatch of whatever took their fancy. It had happened before on more than one occasion

– a teacher's handbag, a tape recorder, etc. Our intrepid deputy head, not the tallest of people, calmly walked up to them as though they were parents attending an open evening, smiled sweetly and said, 'Hello, can I help you?'

Clearly they weren't used to this sort of greeting. Not a 'Clear off!' or 'I'll send for the police!' or even a 'What are you doing here?'. No, it was a very calm, 'Hello, can I help you?'

Thankfully, she got away with it and after a few mumbled comments, the three intruders left quickly through the back doors while Joyce returned, quite unruffled, to join in our final assembly song.

'All things bright and beautiful,
All creatures great…'

Considering our particular patch, things could have turned out far from bright and beautiful but, as with so many who work with children, her personal safety often took second place and was put to the back of her mind.

*

Personal safety was very much to the forefront of my own mind a few weeks after the assembly incident as I knocked on the door of a pupil's house in the school's catchment area. It started on a wet, Monday morning with a boy sent to my office with a sealed note from his teacher. After he handed it over, unaware of its contents, I read the brief phrase: 'Look at the back of his head'.

'That's fine, Stephen. Tell Mrs S. I'll see her about it later.' Stephen turned and walked away from my desk, revealing the back of his thick, black hair that had been shaved in deep, diamond-shaped patterns.

'Just a minute Stephen, before you go.'

He stopped at the door.

'About your hair-style!' I went on to explain that his trendy hair-do wasn't acceptable and that I would have to take him home. Now, I'm not against fashion initiative and inventiveness but I knew our pupils and was quite familiar with the thin end of the wedge scenarios. Let this go and within a few days even more bizarre hairstyles would be cropping up in the school: close-cropped skin-head types, semi-shaved and dyed pink… Pretty much as it is today in some schools – and that's just the staff!

Only a few months earlier a comprehensive school in the town had banned a pupil who had the word 'OXO' shaved into the back of his head. No, it would have to be stopped. Not relishing the forthcoming confrontation, I drove Stephen home.

I had no problems with Stephen; he was a nice lad, our school-team goalie, and seemed to accept my reasoning. He even thought it funny when I suggested that school-team numbers were shaved on the players' heads. He'd had his fun; now I was having mine. There was no need to beat him up over the situation, just play it low key. He had seen the implications, we'd shared a laugh and it had been sorted. If only adults were as easy to deal with; now there was the tricky matter of informing his parents.

On the way to his home, I asked, 'Will your mam be in?'

'Oh yes,' he replied.

We waited outside his door after the third series of knocks. No reply. 'I thought you said your mother would be in.'

As I turned from the door, with the rain falling quite steadily, Stephen commented, 'Sometimes she goes to the shops, but me dad's in. He should be – he's been on night shift!'

Suddenly there was the noise of someone banging down the stairs. This should be fun! There in front of me, wearing trousers only, belt dangling from his waist, tousled hair, sleep and anger in his eyes, was Stephen's dad. Naturally he was not overjoyed to see us or delighted at being disturbed! 'Yes?' he growled. I would have growled too.

I told him why we were on his doorstep and, in spite of his tiredness, he conceded that the haircut was rather severe. Actually Stephen's dad was very good about the whole situation but, in the main, most parents are if you are honest and straightforward with them. As for the hairstyle, the pattern grew out within a few days with the help of some severe grooming, I suspect. The lad returned and played in goal for the school the following Saturday. I was hoping his dad would be on the touchline to watch the match as I wanted to thank him for being so reasonable. Also, in fun, I wanted to add, 'I've brought a goalkeeper's cap, just in case!'

It's always nice to have supportive parents and it has never failed to amaze me how loyal they can be when it comes to sport, especially football. Over the years they've sanded pitches in the winter, provided welcome refreshments, erected goalposts, transported children to games, bought football strips and even taken time off work to watch important games. Many of these keen parents, mainly dads, would not have been seen dead at formal open evenings but chatted away quite freely while standing on the touchline or while their children were getting changed for a match.

Certainly the discussions I've had proved useful and productive in helping with their children's all-round education and promoting good relationships.

*

During the last season of sport before I retired, I experienced a most unusual and mind-boggling journey all in the name of school football. We had been drawn in the Cleveland County Cup against a school in a place called Dormanstown, near the coastal resort of Redcar-by-the-Sea. Rather than travel in a minibus, we decided to use five cars to ferry the pupils the journey of twenty miles.

When we started out on our excursion, the sky was rather grey and leaden but, ever hopeful, we bundled into our cars and drove off towards the East Cleveland area. As we approached Middlesbrough, the rain started to drizzle steadily and our car lights were needed in the gathering gloom though it was only mid-afternoon.

Our route took us through a depressing industrial landscape via steelworks and factories, so the rain had a backdrop of smoke, occasional flames from chimney stacks and grimy buildings. Then the heavy thunder and lightning started, great flashes across the sky accompanied with the rolling thunderstorms. Even more rain lashed down and the noise was deafening; it was almost completely dark save for the car headlights, the flash of fire from the chimney stacks and lightning streaks. Our speed was restricted to a crawl for safety reasons and so that we could stay in convoy. Most of the traffic on the Middlesbrough to Redcar trunk road was doing the same.

We pressed on through this nightmare Dante's Inferno experience and eventually reached our destination, parking in the playground, which was awash with water.

Plodging through the puddles, I entered the school building and was greeted by the surprised sports teacher in a deserted hall. The pitch on which we were to play, as he indicated through the window, was by now a lake and only fit for aquatic sports. Plans were made to play the fixture the following week and I returned to our party. As I approached my car one of our boys, ever the optimist, had managed to get himself changed into his school kit and wound the window down, shouting, 'Are we playing, sir?'

I did not reply but sat down in my moist track suit and aquaplaned back to home base with the group. 'I'll miss all these joys when I retire,' I thought.

Little did I realise how soon this retirement would be. It was due to a combination of factors, the overriding reason being that my wife was not enjoying the best of health at the time, which led her to be very poorly.

Since the days of 1966, I had given one hundred per cent to my work; my mind was locked into school life and events within the establishment. But, to quote the legendary Dylan, 'the times they were a changin'', or in my case about to change.

A few months prior to my decision to go, I was ill due to overwork and the stress and strain of trying to cope with home events and school. I suppose my efforts over the years, non-stop at times, had taken their toll. In hindsight, a wonderful thing, I should have tried to pace myself better but such was my nature that I doubt it would have worked for me. Whatever, my decision was made one day and with apprehensive feelings I filled in the form, met with the people from personnel and prepared to be de-mobbed.

September of 1996 arrived (how thirty years have flown) like any other and there was no thought in my mind that I would not complete the school year. Indeed, had someone told me I would leave the following Easter I would have laughed out loud; but Easter came and I departed, having tied up as many loose ends as possible before the wrench of locking up my desk and leaving my keys for the last time.

*

What a massive store of memories I took away with me. So many individuals, so many lives that I had, in my own small way, helped to build and shape.

As the week of my departure grew nearer, every annual or termly routine task, whether of an administrative nature or with staff and pupils, made me think, 'That's the last time I'll be doing this.' What a sad individual I was turning into! Of course, even in the countdown to my leaving, it was never a case of free-wheeling; it's just not like that in any primary school. The children are there, in your face as the current expression goes, and their needs, demands and challenges cannot be put to one side. Take your foot off the gas at your peril!

Perhaps the thing that put my retirement into sharp focus was seeing my position advertised in the local education circular and dates pencilled in for prospective head teachers to view the school, attend interview and be appointed. Speculation was rife: who could they find to fill the shoes of this revered fellow? Well, I could think of several thousand, but the choice was limited to three!

In turn the appointment was made – a lady. Problems! We would have to change the masculine decor in my room, get rid of the muddy football boots in the corner, the football league fixture list on the pin board and the West Hartlepool Rugby Club pennant (sorry Rovers!) flapping from the ceiling. In with the flowered wallpaper, chintz curtains and the vase of flowers! Sexist – who me?

I jest, just as my head-teacher colleagues did with their humorous remarks. Yes, I would miss them too, a great bunch of special people, most of whom I could ring any time, assured of their support and guidance. I wonder what is the collective noun for head teachers? An ache of heads? A report of heads?

But those I would miss most were the children and staff of the school. One of the great joys in the teaching profession is to see children move along their journey through school, seeing how over the weeks and years confidence is gained, new skills acquired and often the most amazing transformations take place. We can't wave a magic wand, and we all have our struggles with certain pupils, but there are few schools that do not have their success stories of children who were difficult to manage in their early years and yet, through hard work, sheer persistence and dedication by staff (teaching and non-teaching), have left their school as first-class pupils. When this happens, I find there is nothing more rewarding; every minute of toil and trial on behalf of the school is worth it. Perhaps that is the reason why, when everything seemed an uphill task, many teachers I have known took a deep breath, dusted themselves down and came back for more.

Staff would also be missed, as they were in all the schools in which I have taught. So many characters over the years. My yardstick was always 'Would you like your own sons and daughters to be taught by them?' I'm not going to be so sentimental and patronising as to say 'oh yes, I would', but in the majority of cases I'd be more than happy for this to happen.

*

So the end of Memory Lane is in sight. Let me finish with tales that brought tears to my eyes, both happy and sad.

The first story concerns an ex-colleague talking to a girl at her desk about a school record form. My colleague was seeking information about the child's family and was part way through the form.

'Right, Julie, that's your address. Now, what's your mam's name?'

'Angela,' replied the pupil.

'Oh, that's a nice name. Now what's your dad's name?'

'I don't know.'

'Are you sure?' coaxed my colleague. 'Come on, Julie, what does your mam call your dad?'

'A bad bugger, Miss!'

Of course the second tale has to be a soccer story, one that encapsulates all the very best in school football. It's about a boy scoring goals for his school team against very weak opponents; one, then two, then three goals he scores – hey, that's a hat-trick! On he goes to score two more, five goals in all. As the final whistle is about to be blown, he moves in towards the hapless keeper, skilfully rounds him and shoots wide of the open goal. He's missed!

After the match, the hero is congratulated, especially by his dad who was proudly watching on the touch-line.

'Brilliant, son, a great performance. But how did you miss right at the end? If you had scored it would have been a double hat-trick! Not many footballers manage that.'

'Well,' replied his son, 'I had a good game, Dad, and enjoyed scoring. At the end I got past the keeper and I could have scored but…'

'But what, son?' asked his dad.

'But the goalkeeper was crying!'

*

My room during the hectic final week was like Piccadilly Circus, with so many ex-pupils, ex-staff and ex-anyone else associated with the school visiting to voice their own personal goodbyes. I did not realise how many folk were overjoyed at my departure! Joyce, my deputy, was also leaving; she was well loved and respected and that brought in far many more well-wishers.

Nice things were said to us both during our dual-leaving do. Joyce made a lovely speech and I said a few words and read a poem (to quote Morecambe and Wise)'what I wrote the night before'.

The thing that I like most of all,
Is Friday teatime in the hall.
Long past the bell and cries of home,
The hustling, bustling children gone.
Footmarks scuffed near entrance door,
And silence not heard, days before.

The time for dreams of what could be,
Go through my mind, yet stay with me.
Children smart and clean and bright,
Rows of sums, all ticked, all right!
Stories written, punctuated,
Plots completed, well created.

Books all neat and straight and stacked,

Paint pots clean and trays all racked.
Pencils sharpened, lids on tins,
Boards all clean, rubbish in bins.
No one absent, no one late,
Leavers all left, through the gate.

Songs all sung with merry voice,
Lunches cooked with perfect choice.
'Lines' all straight and entrance same,
Teams outstanding, every game.
Parents always full of praise,
No lack of sun, no 'rainy' days.

No missing end of sellotape,
No playground hassle, cuts or scrape.
Pens on tables, coats on hooks,
No missing chairs and likewise books.
Keys in locks, no missing links,
Plugs unplugged from all the sinks.

Toilet paper in the loo,
Hand towels doing what hand towels do.
Flushing toilets, channels free,
'Scenty' smells, no hint of pee!
Mondays few, all training days,
Assemblies full of thanks and praise.

Teachers healthy, always here,
Problem children, none I fear!
I've taught so many from four to eleven,
But not in this place, it must be Heaven!

Hardly worthy of a literary prize but it was my take on dreams of a perfect school situation.

So, as I end my book, my school journey comes to an end, gathering pace as a spinning coin then suddenly flat. That was it, done and dusted!

*

Easter holidays arrived and disappeared. Thus beckoned days of passing my time, doing the dusting around the house, ironing, popping round to the shops for a few groceries, watching the occasional afternoon black-and-white movie...

Brrr...brrr...brrr... 'Hello, Mr Cross speaking.'

'Oh hello, this is "St Desperate to Get a Teacher Primary School". You couldn't help us out, could you? We are looking for a supply teacher for the next two or three days and we heard you were available.'

I wonder who 'grassed me up'! If they think I'm going back to work in school then...

'Right, well, just a minute. I'll have a word with my wife.'

8

DEMAND AND SUPPLY

'THIS IS MR CROSS, HE USED TO BE IMPORTANT!'

Year 5 primary pupil

Many are the times I have read the poems and stories of Spike Milligan to pupils. A two-line verse that springs to mind is Spike's version of John Masefield's classic, 'Sea Fever' which reads:

I must go down to the sea again, to the lonely sea and the sky.

I left my shoes and socks there, I wonder if they're dry?

With great apologies to Masefield and Milligan, may I offer my own humble version, appropriate to this final chapter:

I must go back to the school again, to the bell and the playground cry.

The teacher's still inside of me, I think I'll try supply.

So, after a whole summer term and summer holiday, I found myself back in harness once more. To be truthful, I believe my wife needed a few days a week respite from my school withdrawal symptoms! But could I manage, back in front of a class? Well, of course; hadn't I taken quite a few classes as a head? Yes, but this was a wee bit different. As head, I could counter the awkward pupils with such lines as, 'Hmm young man/lady, this won't do. I think you may have to see the head teacher after school, but I'm sure there'll be no need for that as you'll settle down to work before the end of the lesson!' It worked – sometimes.

Of course, as a supply teacher I was unknown in each new school. I couldn't hide behind the authority I'd previously known. I was a shell-less winkle. The pupils didn't know me from Adam – I was a stranger from outer space! It certainly was a challenge; indeed on meeting an ex-head colleague, he laughed at my new-found role and with a chuckle remarked, 'Well, can you still hack it then?'

Hack it? Who, me? I was the best hacker in the business! Without doubt it was no easy ride; in fact I often had to call upon every ounce of my years of experience to cope. It made me realise as never before how difficult it is for newly qualified teachers not to secure a permanent position and have to start their career on the supply list.

*

Starting off again filled me with great fear and uncertainty. How would staff react to an ex-head on supply? Would they think he knew it all? (I wish!). Would they think he was an expert? I hoped not, as I'd heard a definition of the word 'ex': a has-been, and 'spurt': a drip under pressure! What about the heads of the schools? Would they feel uncomfortable with me around?

Well, the staff were fine in all the schools I worked in, probably as they were so darned busy they didn't have time to worry about the old boy working alongside them! There were tricky moments when certain heads were criticised within the staffroom (actually that's what these rooms are for!); but there may have been times when I was the focus of my staff's uncomplimentary remarks when I was head. (Never!)

At such delicate moments when it was head-bashing time, I would often 'need' a toilet visit. They must have thought I had the weakest bladder in the whole of the teaching profession!

Months passed by and I recall working with a regular class when we had a visit from a governor. It was customary for each governor of the school to be allocated to a class, I guess to develop good relationships and for links to be made with children's activities and work patterns. This particular morning our pupil guide was explaining some of the projects in which we were involved before turning towards me and saying, 'Oh yes, this is Mr Cross. He used to be important!'

Hey, son, come here! What do you mean 'used to be'? No, really it was so funny. I was aching to burst out laughing but the poor governor looked so serious I had to hold it in.

*

My twilight teaching years were also full of interest and, of course, there were the bus trips. Two, in particular! I love walking, especially on the North Yorkshire Moors, so a hike from Captain Cook's monument to Roseberry Topping during the autumn term was something I really looked forward to.

Cometh the morning and our school party set off on a bright, brisk day, bound for the hills. Soon we were all striding along the well-trodden path with drystone walls on our right and the curved back of Roseberry Topping in front. Alas the drystone wall did not stay dry for too long! Within minutes, as can happen on the moor tops, the weather turned nasty and we were hit by a fierce storm with the rain falling as in the most extreme Hollywood movie! With nowhere to shelter, we plodded on. Few of the group were able to fend off the rain. Most of the staff and children were drenched, cold and struggling against gale-force winds that had turned a pleasant stroll into an appalling experience.

There was no stopping for a packed lunch, there was no stopping for a rest, there was no stopping, full stop! Let's get back to the car park at Newton-under-Roseberry and get back to school and home! Slipping and sliding into the car park, soaked to the skin, we had the welcome sight of the double-decker bus awaiting our departure. Then, as we were approaching our escape vehicle, a lady member of staff who had been first to reach the bus walked back to the main group of bedraggled hikers and greeted us with the numbing words: 'The bus has broken down!'

What a bad time for silly jokes, I thought. Can't she see that we've had enough? Yes, she can see that. No, she isn't joking!

The bus had indeed broken down; the engine wouldn't start. There was no heating on the bus, just forty to fifty soaking-wet pupils plus seven or eight staff; things were not looking too rosy.

As we waited for almost an hour, lids of packed lunch boxes came off, ring pulls were taken off cans, food and drinks were consumed as the dripping wet passengers sought some kind of relief. The pupils were a credit and as resilient as only children can be, whilst the staff did their best to keep up the spirits of all the party. The body warmth of so many packed pupils created a thin mist, which rose towards the bus ceiling.

Me, I didn't eat. I was in a state of shock, sitting there frozen, tired and thinking, 'Did I really miss all this?'

Stubbornly refusing offers of a variety of crisps, biscuits and a weird array of goodies that parents manage to conjure up to stuff inside a plastic box, I sat there like a real grouch. Usually on occasions like this, I try to jolly along the youngsters but for some strange reason I just sat there like a veritable Mr Glum. Maybe it was just a bridge too far; I had been on hundreds of outings in the past and there were quite a few still to come, but I've yet to fathom out why on this occasion I felt so dismal and downbeat. It certainly was the soaking, even though as I drove home after a period of almost two hours, parts of my clothing were still rather moist!

Stepping inside the back door at home and peeling off my clothes in the kitchen area, I disappeared up the stairs dressed in damp boxer shorts and ankle socks, aware of a shake of my wife's head and the words, 'Well, I did warn you!'

If this was a nightmare trip, another that followed shortly afterwards ran a close second, although on this occasion I remained in good spirits in spite of the grim events. We had spent a delightful day walking in the countryside, taking a route past an airfield, skirting the famous hillside White Horse and ending up in the Kilburn village of 'Mousey Thompson' fame. This time the school group boarded the bus having enjoyed their day and looking forward to a restful return journey, a few 'silly' songs on the coach ride home, pupils showing off their treasures bought from the village gift shop...

'Do you think my mam will like this, sir?'

'Oh, I'm sure.' Well, sure – if your mam likes grotesque little ornaments on her mantelpiece. Am I being cynical here?

...maybe one or two drifting off to sleep.

Wrong, this was not the pattern of this day. The bus engine was perfect but the bus driver was not so perfect – in fact, he lost his way! We ended up driving miles and miles down narrow country roads, not only winding from side to side but up and down. Children full of food and drink, excited, hot and sweaty, bus moving all over the place – I think you have guessed the result. Yes, you've got it in one. VOMIT!

Some of you may be familiar with a local bus company that I believe is still operating called OK Travel. This should have had 'Not So OK' on the side or maybe 'Vomit Bus'. I'm not averse to a bit of sickness on school travel; indeed, over the years I've experienced quite a bucketful. I well recall travelling with a junior youth club group when a little girl sitting next to me turned and was sick all over me. (Sorry if you're about to have tea!)

Thus said, my sickness credentials are quite impressive so I speak with a great deal of knowledge when I say this journey from Kilburn to Teesside was a high-ranking, pupil-to-school-trip ratio of vomiting! I will not elaborate much further but the statistics were such that those who were sick reached double figures! Every bag, every paper towel, every grain of sawdust was used from the 'every school trip has one' sick box.

I am a firm believer that good can be found in most experiences of life; in this case the bus driver, who had the task of cleaning up the mess we couldn't take with us. Surely in future he would make sure that he knew the route back and forth, no matter where he was travelling.

*

These occasions were, I'm glad to say, quite rare. Of the hundreds of school outings by coach, including weekly runs to the swimming baths, trips to sports events and visits to places as a link with curricular activities, most of them passed by without any serious mishaps. In leaving this school-trip section of school life I must finish with a delightful tale, in the main due to a typical childlike comment, which made me smile.

Not only did this visit end with a coach ride back to school but it began with a walk before boarding a boat to cruise down the River Tees from Stockton to Preston Park.

It was a lovely day, no river-sickness, a walk round the park and, to finish, the children ate an outdoor picnic sitting in the middle of the vast expanse of flat grassland that is one of the main areas of the park. They were of a young primary age, six or seven years old.

Waiting for the bus to take us back to school, one little girl asked, 'Can we play some games?'

'Of course,' replied her teacher. 'What would you like to play?'

'Hide and seek!'

The teacher raised her arm and, with palm outstretched, turned around in a circle to indicate the flatness hundreds of yards on every side. Scratching her head the tiny girl, with a puzzled expression on her face and letting out a bewildered sigh as the penny dropped, said, 'Oh no, miss! There's nowhere to hide!'

Yet another treasure in the memory bank! My final year as a part-timer ended and I left with many gems that cost so very little but in some ways were priceless.

So, these bonus supply-teaching days eased me into full time retirement after more than forty years working in schools.

What a joy it has been working with so many varied characters, young and old. If you are one of my ex-pupils or ex-staff then thank you so much for putting up with me. It was truly my pleasure and privilege.